Imran Khan

ALL ROUND VIEW

CHATTO & WINDUS

LONDON

Published in 1988 by
Chatto & Windus Ltd
30 Bedford Square
London WC1B 3RP

A CIP catalogue record for this book is available from the British Library

ISBN 0 7011 3330 9
Copyright © Imran Khan 1988

Photoset by Rowland Phototypesetting Ltd
Bury St Edmunds, Suffolk
Printed in Great Britain by
Redwood Burn Ltd
Trowbridge, Wiltshire

Contents

FOR MY MOTHER

Illustrations

Section Six *(between pages 178 and 179)*

Prologue

I had always promised myself that I would leave cricket when I was still at the peak of my form and still enjoying the game. Above all, I vowed that I would never be at the mercy of the selectors, or face the prospect of being kicked out in an undignified way like so many of the Pakistani greats. Ideally I would have liked to leave on a winning note at the end of 1987, but the Australians upset that plan by beating us in the World Cup semi-final at Lahore.

I realised that any player who leaves at his peak faces pressure to come back, particularly if his place hasn't been adequately filled. But I never realised the amount of pressure I was going to face, and that despite Pakistan winning the 1987 series in England. It became still more intense when Javed Miandad quit the captaincy at the end of the series against England in Pakistan. People demonstrated outside my house, and one or two even threatened a hunger strike. My mailbag increased to about a hundred letters a day, and the phone never stopped ringing. I avoided crowded places after I had been told I would be mobbed by people insisting that I come back.

But the real pressure came from the boys in the Pakistan team. Most of them – especially the younger ones – pleaded with me to take them to the West Indies. Some of them were so disillusioned by the way in which the 1987 home series against England had been played, that they were contemplating missing the West Indies series. For the first time I gave some serious thought to a comeback. After all, the boys had stood by me through thick and thin over the past two years. They had given me their complete loyalty: now that they needed me, was it such a big thing for me to change my mind?

Whatever reservations I had were removed by General Zia at a banquet given for the Pakistan team on 18 January 1988. He gave a long speech, the crux of which was that while he appreciated my decision to leave at my peak, and felt it was a good one as far as I was concerned, the country needed me and sometimes 'one had to rise above the *self*'. It was a great honour that the head of state had felt it necessary to appeal to me to join the team.

I have to say here that all my family and close friends thought that I should have stuck to my decision to retire, and that although I had not done so on a winning note, I had left with more dignity than other Pakistani players. They also felt that, in Pakistan, people's attachment to cricket was an emotional affair, and that if I lost in the West Indies they would not appreciate the reason for my taking on such a great challenge. No visiting team had won in the West Indies since 1973. In fact, few teams had even lost decently – for the most part they had been completely destroyed. England had been the last team to tour the Caribbean, and they had lost 5-0. So shell-shocked was that English team that it lost the following summer to India and New Zealand.

However, this safe, no-risk thinking was not me. All my career I have taken risks: how could I forgo a chance of beating the West Indies on their home ground? To do so would result in Pakistan's being recognised for the first time as the best team in the world. I would never forgive myself in years to come if I thought that being scared to lose had made me miss such a unique opportunity.

CHAPTER 1

Beginnings

Both my parents came from Pathan landowning families. My father's tribe, the Niazi, arrived in India when the Lodhi Pathans were ruling in the twelfth and thirteenth centuries. My mother belonged to the Burkis, a Turko-Afghan people who also came from Afghanistan, though they came to India a little later, after a dispute within their tribe. Like all Pathans, the Burkis and the Niazis were extremely proud of their backgrounds and clung on to their identity for hundreds of years.

Independence is a hallmark of the entire Pathan race, and both my parents drummed it into us that we should not be dominated by anyone. They had witnessed the struggle for independence in 1947, and as a student my father had been actively involved in the independence movement. Both were fiercely anti-colonial and – after Pakistan had emerged as an independent Muslim state – patriotic Pakistanis, though my father used to get quite upset by a new class of Pakistani bureaucrats who simply stepped into the shoes of the colonialists and were known as the *Kala sahibs* or black sahibs. The *Kala sahibs* acted out, and even adopted, the ways of the English. I remember how my father used to tick off the waiters in the Lahore Gymkhana Club who spoke to him in English. He also found it weird when Pakistani parents spoke English to their children. But – according to him – the worst type of *Kala sahibs* were those who played or watched polo. It was as though they were playing at Windsor Castle rather than the Lahore Polo Ground, and if anyone spoke Urdu, it was with an English accent.

I

My mother was a strong and proud woman, as were her two sisters. She had strong views on many issues, including politics and religion. Once, when I was thirteen, I was stopped by the police while driving my father's car. I knew I was driving without a licence, so I bribed the policeman and got away with it. The chauffeur reported the incident to my mother. She was furious. She felt stooping to bribery was a real loss of dignity, and that I should have gone to gaol instead. I tried to defend myself by saying that other boys of my age had done the same in similar situations. Her answer was brief: 'You are a Pathan.' In her eyes that was synonymous with pride and honesty.

For as far back as I can remember, I was more ambitious than other boys of my age. As a youth, my confidence in my abilities as a cricketer seemed a natural outcome of the strong cricketing tradition in my family. From the age of seven I lived in Zaman Park – a small, compact, wooded, residential district situated on the right bank of the canal that runs through the heart of modern Lahore. The park there is used throughout the year for sporting activities, and cricket in particular. Before I was ten I was playing with members of my family, some of whom were already first-class cricketers. Zaman Park was the ideal environment for a budding cricketer. I can think of no other small neighbourhood, even in Barbados or the other West Indian islands, that has produced so many good cricketers.

My parents had settled in Zaman Park in the late 1950s. Before that my father was in government service, and we were constantly moving from place to place. Although most of my mother's family lived in what is now India, my maternal grand-uncle, Zaman Khan, lived in Lahore, in the area which was later named after him. In those days Zaman Park consisted of only five or six houses, and was situated on the outskirts of the city. He was the only Muslim inhabitant, the other houses belonging to Hindus. During Partition the Hindu families migrated to India, while my mother's family, travelling in the opposite direction, moved into Zaman Park. These were uncertain and difficult times, and refugees in particular tended to cluster together. Once a few members of the family had settled in Zaman Park, others followed suit.

The cricketing strain in my family comes from my mother's side, and has a long and chequered history. Jahangir Khan, Majid's father, was a Cambridge blue and played Test cricket for India in the 1930s. Majid's brother, Asad, was an Oxford blue, and another relative, Baqa Jilani, played in a Test for India against England at the Oval in 1936. My mother's only brother, Ahmad Raza Khan, was also a renowned first-class cricketer before Partition, captaining Punjab against a touring MCC side. In my mother's family cricket was a passion and the main topic of conversation. When I was a small boy, my mother used to tell me stories about the cricket matches in Jullundur between the men in the family. When the family moved to Lahore after Partition and congregated in Zaman Park, it was only natural that cricket should be the focus of activity.

My mother's first cousin, Javed Zaman, took charge of the sporting activities in Zaman Park. He also captained Lahore Gymkhana, which he does to this day. He has played for thirty years, and can land the ball on a line and length with his eyes closed. He has played a major part in shaping the cricketing talents of two generations of young boys – mine and the present one. He is known as 'the godfather', and it is fitting that he should have assumed this role since his father was the first family member to settle in Zaman Park.

My mother and her two sisters all had sons who went on to captain Pakistan – Javed Burki, Majid and myself. Eight of my cousins have played first-class cricket, largely as a result of the calibre of the cricket played in Zaman Park. Soon after my father moved there I began to take part in matches in the Park. The games were quite remarkable, in that the players were anything between ten and thirty years old: first-class cricketers played with and against youngsters who could only just hold a full-size cricket bat. Yet children and grown-ups alike were extremely serious and competitive in their approach to the game. The cricket was of a high standard, with the result that the youngsters' development was extremely rapid. Occasionally we played 'past' versus 'present' matches, in which all those aged fourteen and under played against the rest; the 'past' players had to bat left-handed and bowl spin. I had to struggle in the early days because, when I first played in Zaman Park at the age of eight, I was not as good as other boys of my age, and was the last to be picked. This put me off cricket for a while – but there was no escaping it, because in Zaman Park all roads led to the cricket field.

It took me a while to catch up with the rest. Naseer Mohammad, the games superintendent at my school, Aitchison College, was largely responsible for turning me round. He took one look at my batting style – which consisted exclusively of cross-batted slogs – and decided I needed a firm lesson in the basics of the game, front- and back-foot defence with a straight bat. After this, my batting improved dramatically, and I was no longer a sitting duck for the bowlers at Zaman Park. As my periods at the crease grew longer, my attitude to the game changed: all I wanted to do was to play cricket. I decided that I was going to play for Pakistan, and soon. To my mind this seemed pretty straightforward. After all, Majid had become a Test cricketer at the age of eighteen: there was no reason, I thought, why I couldn't make it even earlier, particularly since I was already the best batsman in my prep-school team at the age of eleven.

This precocious and naive conviction was the result of my knowing that Javed Burki and Majid Khan had already played for Pakistan. Watching my two elder cousins play in Test matches, I imagined myself striding out, performing great feats with the bat, and pulling Pakistan out of a tight spot. Such childhood fantasies are common enough, but in my case they had the force of reality. When I was just twelve, I went to watch Majid and Javed play New Zealand at Rawalpindi with my uncle Ahmad Raza Khan, a national selector. He told his friends that one day I would play for Pakistan. I never forgot that moment: for me his words were gospel.

4

Throughout my school years the exploits of Javed Burki and Majid Khan formed the framework within which I saw my development as a cricketer. Javed was an established batsman and had already captained Pakistan, but Majid's career exerted the greatest influence on me. Only six years older than I was, he was already a legend in Lahore because of his incredible stroke play and medium-fast bowling. He was the star of Zaman Park and my cricketing idol. Later, when we played together for Pakistan, I used to feel far worse when he was got out than I did about my own dismissals.

Within a couple of years I was, at fourteen, the youngest member of the Aitchison College team. Aitchison is an élite school with a superb cricket ground, one of the most beautiful I've ever seen. I was the school's opening batsman and made a good many runs. At that time I was purely a batsman; no one took my bowling seriously, not even myself. I did my share of bowling in the nets, of course, but rarely bowled in a game. At school I was intent on rewriting the batting records. It was not until I was almost fifteen that I began to bowl more frequently, largely because I enjoyed watching the batsmen hop away from my short-pitched deliveries. I had little interest in taking wickets.

Living and playing in the sequestered upper-class environment of Zaman Park, Aitchison College and Lahore Gymkhana, I had no idea of cricket outside this small and privileged world. Since I was the best batsman at school, I automatically assumed that I was almost certainly better than anyone else of my age in the country. I was included in the trials to select an under-nineteen team that would represent Lahore against a touring English under-nineteen side. Almost two hundred boys turned up, and no one was allowed much time at the crease. The selectors must already have had a clear idea of who was going to play, since it's impossible to judge a batsman's ability in just three or four minutes. I strode out to bat, wearing my newly-acquired spikes and ready to unleash a glittering array of strokes; but the spikes upset my footwork and the first few deliveries beat me completely. The harder I

5

tried, the worse it became, and I was soon told to go and stand in the outfield.

After the regular bowlers had been tried, the selectors asked the all-rounders to have a go. To my amazement, one of the selectors stopped me after a few deliveries and announced that I had the perfect action for a fast bowler. Considering the many years and the hard work it took me subsequently to change my action, I wonder how much he really knew about fast bowling. Anyway, I was selected as a fast bowler and consoled myself with the thought that I would at least have a chance to unveil my prodigious batting talent at number ten!

Under-nineteen cricket was a revelation: it changed my conception of the world and of my own abilities. For the first time I was playing with cricketers who came from totally different backgrounds, some of whom had learned their cricket the hard way — in the streets, on the roadside, on any flat piece of ground, in places like Iqbal Park where ten matches were usually being played at the same time. To begin with I was treated with a certain amount of hostility. My team-mates thought I did not deserve a place in the team and was there on the basis of my connections. For a number of reasons, in particular my inadequate Punjabi — later perfected under Sarfraz's tutorship — I was the target of their jokes and sarcasm. (Punjabi is the language spoken throughout that part of the country, but at home we spoke Urdu.) Only when I had proved myself and had come to understand the difficulties which some of them had had to surmount did a relationship of mutual respect develop. In sharp contrast to my luxurious development, some Pakistani players have had to struggle against almost impossible odds to become the players they are. In the current Pakistani team, for example, Abdul Qadir and Tauseef Ahmed have risen from nowhere, almost like characters in a fairy tale. I also discovered that I had far too high an opinion of my own batting. Wasim Raja, the captain of the under-nineteen side, was in a different class altogether and was already batting with a maturity far beyond his years. Others were also streets ahead of me — such as Afzal Masood, an outstanding schoolboy cricketer, or Azmat Rana, the brother of Shafqat and Shakoor and a natural ball player. I realised that I had been lucky in Lahore not having any fast bowlers, and that my bowling had propelled me into first-class cricket.

I made my first-class debut for Lahore against Sargodha. The chairman of the selectors was my uncle, while the captain of the Lahore side and the senior player were my cousins. Some called this nepotism. I, of course, preferred to regard it as pure coincidence. I then behaved as though I was doing everyone a favour by gracing the occasion. I was to be the opening batsman and the opening bowler, and I was still only sixteen. It rained before the match, and rather than hang around the ground I went back to where I was staying and went to sleep. After a long rest, I returned to find that the game had started and that someone else had gone in to open the innings instead of me. Needless to say, I got hell from the captain, Hammayun Zaman, while the team thought me spoilt and unworthy of being given a chance.

After this one match, the principal of Aitchison College, Abdul Ali Khan, refused to let me play any more first-class cricket while I was still at school, so as soon as I had passed my O-level examinations I switched schools, and resumed first-class cricket. I was lucky in that during the 1970–71 season the Lahore side was captained by my cousin, Javed Burki. He used me intelligently, shielding me when things were going badly and encouraging me at the appropriate times. Thanks to him, I was the second-highest wicket-taker that season among the pacemen. I was often erratic, but sometimes I got everything right – more often than not in the big matches. In March 1971, I was chosen to play for a Pakistan XI against an international XI led by Micky Stewart. I took three wickets, including Stewart twice, and, coming in at number nine, made 51 not out when our side was in danger of being skittled out for a meagre total. My performance in this match was largely responsible for my being included in the squad to tour England that summer. It also prompted Wing Commander William Shakespeare, Worcestershire's chairman, to talk to me about playing for the county. My parents immediately refused, arguing that my education would be interrupted.

Back in 1971 Pakistani players had something of an inferiority complex, in that we had always been thrashed in England. We had only won a single Test match in England, in 1954, and that was considered a fluke. When we arrived, the English team was thought to be invincible. Talaat Ali once asked a senior player if it was possible to see the ball once it had left Alan Ward's hand, while another senior player told us not to bother to look back but to walk straight back to the pavilion since Englishmen never dropped a catch. I was told that it would be impossible for me to take any wickets because the English were so perfect technically that there was never any gap between bat and pad, while Zaheer was informed that with such a high back-lift he would find it impossible to get any runs in England.

Nor were our feelings of inferiority confined to the cricket field. In our manager's speech at the MCC dinner he declared that the English had taught us discipline through cricket, and how to eat with a knife and fork. I was too embarrassed to listen to the rest. Some of the players who had been playing league and county cricket in England urged us to do as the English did. It was quite a shock to be reprimanded by other players for ticking off a rude waiter. It was not done in England. I was also told that if I wanted to bowl a lot, I should drink beer like Fred Trueman. I took up milk instead, which even today I find the greatest sustenance. I'm proud to say that the younger players in Pakistan have all followed my example, and far from building up their strength by drinking beer, they have taken up milk instead; yet before the 1971 tour it was considered trendy to drink alcohol on English or Australian tours.

That trip to England was not only my first cricketing tour but my first time out of Pakistan. For an eighteen-year-old schoolboy the excitement of going abroad with the national team was too much. I felt I needed far more than twenty-four hours in each day. It was a time of discovery, both on and off the field. It was such a pleasure to play on the green, well-kept county grounds, with proper pavilions and excellent dressing-room facilities. The pitches and playing areas were beautifully cared for – something I'd not known before. Off the field, I was completely dazzled by the shops, restaurants, cinemas and discos, and I was bent on discovering everything in the quickest possible time.

I came to England brimming with confidence, but ran into problems during my first net practice. I had developed a slinging action, somewhat similar to that of Australia's Jeff Thomson, only wilder. On English pitches I could not bowl accurately at all. The softness of the ground ruined my run-up and I could not get an adequate foothold at the point of delivery. I rarely managed to get the ball anywhere near the stumps. When I did, I found that my two major weapons, the bouncer and the inswinger, were treated with disdain. On English wickets the ball didn't skid off the wicket as it did on Pakistani ones, and my short-pitched deliveries were either cannon-fodder for the batsmen or posed no threat at all to those who refused to play the hook shot. Nor was my stock ball, the inswinger, any problem to the county batsmen, who simply played forward and smothered the swing. In Pakistan, the tendency to play across the line had brought me many easy wickets, but in England wickets were as rare as gold dust. I noticed that when Jeff Thomson first came to England, in 1975, he had similar problems: he overstepped the crease a lot, was inaccurate, and found that the short-pitched delivery which had destroyed English batsmen in Australia was quite manageable in England. It's a case of horses for courses, and the Pakistani team quickly realised that in bringing me with them they had picked a skittish colt who was quite incapable of making the necessary adjustments.

Fortunately for me, and unfortunately for Pakistan, I played in the first Test at Edgbaston because Salim Altaf and Sarfraz Nawaz were both unfit. On the morning of the Test I asked Majid, who was up at Cambridge and only available for the

Test matches, to help me with my run-up. When, in the nets, he saw me casually walking back, turning and running in to bowl he asked me how I actually measured my run-up. I told him that I relied on my judgment, at which he gave me a strange look and told me to carry on bowling.

My baptism in Test cricket was mercifully postponed for two days by Zaheer Abbas, who made 274. When England went in to bat they faced a total of 608 for 7, with the ball really swinging in the cloudy atmosphere. Asif Masood opened the bowling and dismissed Edrich for nought in the first over. From the other end I came on to bowl to the incoming batsman, Colin Cowdrey. My first four deliveries were swinging full-tosses, after which I kept the wicket-keeper, Wasim Bari, at full stretch on the leg side. Intikhab Alam, my captain, kindly explained that an inswinger should start outside the off stump – as if I wasn't trying to do just that. I simply couldn't control the huge swing I was getting. Unfortunately none of England's top-order batsmen – apart from Edrich, who was already out – was left-handed! Despite perfect conditions for swing bowling, I didn't get a single wicket. Asif Masood bowled beautifully, and only a day lost to rain prevented us from going one up in the series. Had he had any support from the other end, not even the weather could have saved England.

Being one of the youngest members of the team brought its own problems. Whenever the team had a bad day on the field, new rules were drawn up at the team meetings. However, if a curfew was declared for the entire team, it was only actually enforced on us younger players. I had known Talaat Ali and Azmat Rana from the Lahore under-nineteen days, and as the three youngest players we were singled out for special treatment. Ours were always the first – and often the only – rooms to be checked. On one occasion we stuffed pillows in our beds and went off to the disco. Unfortunately at the disco we bumped into a couple of senior players who reported us, and we were fined £2 each. In 1971 that was a lot of money, still more so since the end-of-tour bonus for the three of us was £2 each (the others got between £60 and £80). Another time Talaat and I were fined after going with Azmat to Piccadilly Circus. Azmat couldn't speak or write much English. On our way back we got into the Underground; just as the doors were about to close Talaat Ali and I jumped out, leaving a panic-stricken Azmat on the train. About four hours later he was escorted back to the hotel by police. The team manager did not appreciate our prank and we were fined.

On another occasion I was almost sent back to Pakistan. I was sharing a room in Swansea with Saeed Ahmed, the most senior team member. Anxious to impress such an eminent cricketer, I got ready for bed at 10 p.m. He then asked me why I was going to sleep so early, and whether I felt all right. At my age, he told me, he never slept at all: there was a good disco near the hotel and I should go out and enjoy myself. I couldn't believe my ears and thought what a great guy he was and how all the nasty things I'd heard about him were obviously untrue. So I hopped in the Top Rank at Swansea until it closed, and crept back to bed and slept like a baby. A couple of days later we left for Manchester to play at Old Trafford. When we arrived our manager called me over and told me that had it not been for my family he would have sent me home. He said that Saeed had told him how I had woken him up at 3 a.m. every night, and that was why he hadn't scored any runs. Other team members told me later that he had set me up because he wanted a single room.

I had more trouble on account of Mr Ahmed when he burst into tears during a match after a number of catches had been dropped off his bowling. Watching a grown-up bawling his head off, Talaat, Azmat and I could not suppress our laughter. We were hauled up in front of the captain, Intikhab Alam. While he was telling us off Talaat had a giggling fit which set off Azmat and me. Intikhab held his head in his hands and told us to get out.

The more we were treated like schoolboys, the more we behaved like them. Batting at number ten against Northants, I took part in a crucial partnership with the number eleven batsman, Salim Altaf. Salim pulled a muscle, and Talaat Ali was sent in as his runner. This was disastrous. He began to take extremely risky singles despite repeated cautions from Salim. The partnership became highly entertaining because we ran for everything. We only survived by sheer luck. I was eventually run out when Talaat had called for a single after the ball had gone straight to leg slip. We lost the match and got hell from the dressing-room.

As the baby of the team I had a real problem in dealing with the senior players. I was expected to be subservient and to be the butt of most jokes, but not to retaliate. This was difficult, especially since I was better educated than a lot of the other players. Once Asif Masood threatened to beat me up when, having been introduced to a lady at Buckingham Palace as the baby of the team, I introduced him as its Omar Sharif. I was thought too cheeky, but anyone was allowed to say anything to me. Sadiq Mohammad once reported me to the manager because I told him that I was not his servant when he asked me to get him a cup of tea.

England narrowly won the rubber when they beat us by just 25 runs in the third and final Test at Headingley. After the first Test, my contribution was limited to a few county matches. By the end of the tour I had had some sort of fight with most of the players in the team. I was considered a failure after the first Test, so I was treated like any young player who was cocky and felt he was smart, yet was no good at the game. By the end of that tour I felt very isolated and lonely. However, I learned a lot from the experience – most importantly, that if one wanted to be treated with respect by the team, one had to be good at cricket. Moreover, one had to curb one's pride and do odd things like filling the bath for weary bowlers in order to prove that one was part of the team. Remembering my own experiences, I knew how to deal with junior players when I became captain, and made sure they were never neglected as Talaat, Azmat and I had been. Rules should not only apply to young players, and if they do badly a captain should not blame it all on their nocturnal activities.

I had lost all my cockiness and learned the hard way that I was just another raw, inexperienced cricketer. Had I gone back to Pakistan after the tour I might have become just another entry in the long list of one-match wonders that litter the short history of Pakistani cricket. Luckily for me, however, before the first Test Worcestershire had repeated their interest in signing me and we had reached a verbal agreement to satisfy my parents. They had arranged for my admission as a boarder at Worcester Royal Grammar School, where I could take my A-level exams and then try to get into Oxford or Cambridge. Meanwhile I could also play county cricket the following summer.

CHAPTER 2

Winter in England

I spent my first English winter at Worcester Royal Grammar School. I had first felt homesick when the team went back to Pakistan in the middle of July, but when the winter set in I really began to miss Lahore and my family. It was hard enough getting back to my studies after a long lay-off, and I was trying to finish a two-year course in just nine months, but I think it was the English winter rather than the strange environment that got me down so. Worst of all were the dark skies and the constant drizzle, still more so since winter in Pakistan has the best weather of the year. The only good thing was that the weather was conducive to studying, as I hated going outdoors. For the first time in my life I was experiencing short days and no sunshine. I particularly remember being hungry for so much of the time. After lunch on my first day I was already waiting for dinner, and when I felt completely famished I asked when it would be. I almost died when I was told that tea basically consisted of bread, and that what they called dinner was what I called lunch! Since I was used to three cooked meals a day, I had no option but to patronise a shop near the school.

Three months after starting at Worcester RGS I began to bowl again in the school gymnasium, trying to improve my action. I wasn't getting anywhere until the New Zealander, John Parker, suggested that I take a small jump before delivering the ball so as to get more side-on. Although he wasn't impressed by my efforts and suggested that I revert to my original style, I persevered. My action improved, my run-up became more rhythmic and I found I could bowl the occasional leg-cutter. As a result I approached my first county season in England with a little less trepidation.

When playing second-eleven cricket for Worcestershire, the senior county players were unimpressed by my bowling, although my batting won some praise. Glenn Turner in particular thought I would never be a fast bowler. I languished in the second team, where I found the cricket dull and uninspiring. The two men who had signed me had left the county, and the new management had not only registered John Parker ahead of me but reduced my wages. Since the county could not register another overseas player, I now had to get into Oxford – which would entitle me to automatic registration – or go back to Pakistan.

Luckily, even if my stay at Worcester had done nothing for my cricket, it had done enough for my A-level grades to get me into Oxford. I entered Keble College in 1972, and started playing for Oxford University in 1973.

After school, Oxford was wonderful, education in the complete sense. Apart from the studies (the quality of which is undisputed) there was so much more one could do there. There were so many societies to join and so many things to do that the eight-week term seemed far too short. It was while I was at Oxford that I first became aware of the English class system. In Pakistan class seems more clearly defined whereas in England it seems subtler, at least to an outsider.

What I enjoyed most at Oxford was the cricket. The atmosphere was similar to that in which I had grown up, and which I had always enjoyed. Cricket was played competitively, but it was meant to be enjoyed and was never treated as work. The boys were of similar ages and educational backgrounds, so getting along with them was easy, whereas when I played professional cricket – except for one or two short periods in Pakistan and at Sussex – I very rarely found other players with the same approach to the game, if only because our backgrounds and age groups were so varied. My first year at the Parks was one of the most enjoyable ever, even though – from time to time – my studies were inevitably affected by my cricket.

I opened the bowling for the university and batted at number four. Oxford's bowling resources were limited, so I had the chance to put in some long spells. At Worcester, where I played in the second half of the season, I was still considered an erratic batsman and a stock medium-pace bowler – just about an all-rounder.

In 1974 I was elected captain of Oxford. This was my first experience of captaincy at any level, and I found that the responsibility improved my cricket greatly. I hit a hundred in each innings against Nottinghamshire, 160 and 49 against the Indian tourists and 170 against Northants in a match which we won. As for my bowling, I was once again trying to bowl fast. At Worcester, my efforts at fast bowling were looked on with scorn, and I had been bullied into bowling medium-pace line-and-length stuff which didn't suit my temperament. As Oxford's strike bowler, I was free to follow my natural instincts, particularly as we needed some form of retaliation against the liberal dose of bouncers which our batsmen were receiving.

My form at Oxford led to my being included in the Pakistani team that was to tour England in the latter part of the 1974 season. By now I thought of myself as a high-order batsman who could bowl, and this was how I was regarded on the county circuit. I felt that, despite my extra pace and improved control with the ball, my original idea of myself as a cricketer was being vindicated after what had been no more than a brief detour.

The Pakistan selectors had different ideas about my role in the team. Our batting line-up was so strong that there was no question of my batting above number seven or eight. I was chosen for all three Tests, as the third seamer behind Sarfraz and Asif Masood, and as a competent lower-order batsman. I was used as a stock bowler, in which capacity I put in long spells and got a few wickets. In the first Test at Leeds I batted well in a crisis in both innings. In a low-scoring match

I made 23 and 31, and helped the tail to put on almost a hundred runs for the last four wickets in each innings. My overall performance on the tour had been adequate, and there was no longer any reason for my being thought of as a passenger in the side; yet snide remarks were still being made about my connections, and statements to the effect that better players had been left behind in Pakistan. My age and background, and the publicity I got as an Oxford player, probably created some resentment. Nonetheless, despite the occasional carping, I enjoyed the tour. We had a good, competitive team that went through the tour unbeaten. Although all three Tests were drawn, we demolished the counties and swept the one-day internationals.

In 1975 I gave up the Oxford captaincy to concentrate on my final exams, which coincided with the first World Cup. I was selected for the World Cup squad and was expected to play in the last of the group matches if we made it to the semi-finals and the finals. I was asked to play against the Australians on a Saturday, and I still had three papers left on Monday and Tuesday. I left for Leeds on Friday after my exams and got there at 4 a.m. on Saturday. I played the match, with hardly any practice, and was back in Oxford at 3 a.m. Not surprisingly, I got 'flu. On Tuesday one of the outstanding World Cup matches took place between Pakistan and the West Indies, with Pakistan losing by one wicket; my interest quickly switched from my papers to the cricket, for I was desperately anxious to qualify for the semi-finals. Unfortunately, we lost to the West Indies, and were eliminated.

My three years at Oxford were both useful and detrimental to my development as a cricketer. I missed three Test series and most of the first World Cup, nor did I take part in our domestic cricket seasons, with the result that I ended up playing far less international and first-class cricket than I might have done, which undoubtedly hindered my progress as a fast bowler. On the other hand, playing for Oxford renewed my belief in my abilities at a time when my confidence was at its lowest. More importantly, I acquired the ability to think logically, and this helped me to analyse both my own game and cricket in general. I guess the advantages outweighed the disadvantages simply because what I gained was real, and whatever I might have lost is purely conjectural.

I had a miserable season with the bat for Worcestershire in 1975, averaging about ten runs. I couldn't play the hook shot, a serious shortcoming for an attacking batsman. As a fast bowler, a Pakistani and an Oxbridge graduate, I received more than my share of bouncers. Over the years I've noticed that county bowlers are always keen to bowl bouncers at university players. It's a way of putting them in their place.

When I returned to Pakistan in the winter of 1975 I was determined to learn the hook shot, which was even more vital at home. In Pakistan the ball doesn't swing much after the shine has gone, and even medium-pacers resort to two or three bouncers an over. I found a simple and effective method of practising the stroke. I asked a young member of the Lahore Gymkhana staff called Hanif to throw bouncers at me in the nets from a distance of fifteen yards. For half an hour each day I did nothing but practise the hook shot. I had a lot of narrow escapes, the ball missing my head by inches on numerous occasions. In a couple of months I had learned how to cope with the short-pitched delivery.

My bowling also developed in the right direction. In England one could pitch the ball up and let conditions do the rest, but in Pakistan this wasn't enough as there is no movement off the seam. This meant bowling fast and straight. I was the highest wicket-taker in the domestic season, and man of the series in a short 'unofficial' Test series in Sri Lanka.

Back in England in April, for the 1976 season, I felt a lot more confident of my batting and bowling. This was reflected in the very first county match, against Warwickshire, where I made 143 on a fast pitch against an attack that included Bob Willis. Worcestershire promptly confirmed my place at number four in the batting order. My success as a batsman also allowed me to shake off the medium-pace straitjacket into which Worcestershire had stuffed me. Until then my place in

1. A Punjab team: front row left is my mother's cousin, Baqa
   Jilani; third from the left is Majid's father, Jahangir Khan, on his
   left is Agha Ahmad Raza Khan, my mother's brother

2. With my parents and my sisters, Robina and Noreen (on my
   mother's knee)

3. With my mother's cousin, Javed Zaman, who played such an important part in Zaman Park cricket

4. Aitchison College Colts team, 1964

5. Lahore under-nineteen team. It includes the future Pakistan Test players Wasim Raja (*back row, fourth from left*) and Azmat Rana (*back row, far right*)

6. Practising in the nets at Lord's before the 1971 tour of England. Watching me is the tour manager

7. Batting against Hampshire

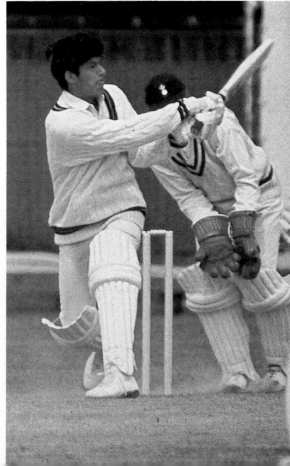

8. Being introduced to the Queen. Azmat is laughing because the captain, Intikhab, has forgotten my name

9. At Worcester Royal Grammar School

10. Batting for Worcester, 1973

11. Bowling to the Indian opener, Naik, at the Parks, Oxford, while playing for the combined Oxford and Cambridge Universities XI, 1974

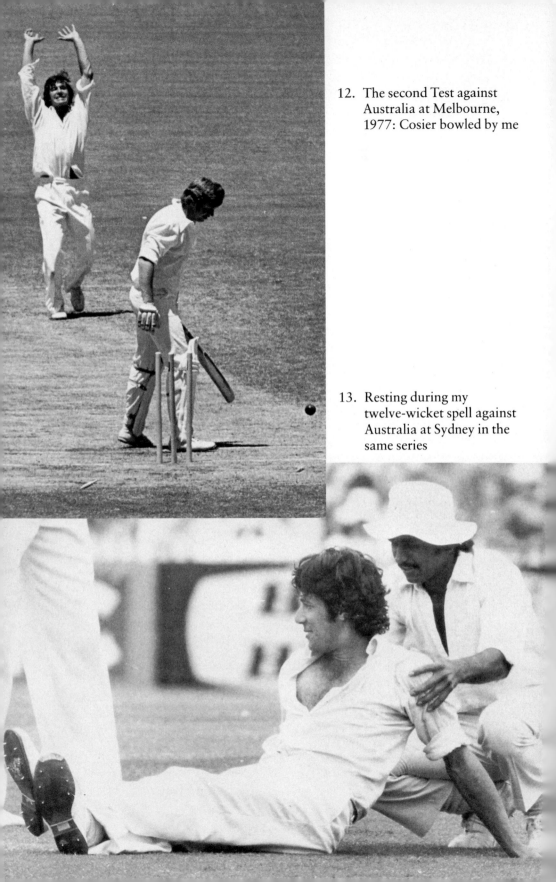

12. The second Test against Australia at Melbourne, 1977: Cosier bowled by me

13. Resting during my twelve-wicket spell against Australia at Sydney in the same series

14. Karachi, 1978. After flying home from Australia, Zaheer, Mushtaq and I weren't selected for the Test against England because we were Packer players

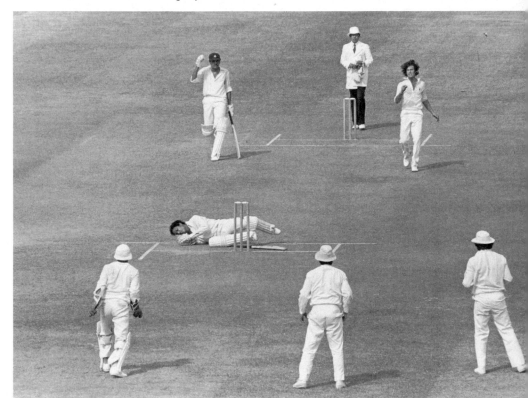

15. The second Test against India at Lahore, 1978. Alas, these were pre-helmet days: Amarnath ducked into a bouncer

16, 17. Melbourne, 1981. The third Test against Australia. Dennis
Lillee is hit by a short-pitched delivery, but still congratulates
me on becoming Pakistan's leading wicket-taker in Tests

the team had depended on my performance as a stock bowler, and I had no option but to bowl inswingers off a run-up of seven or eight paces. In 1976 I decided to ignore instructions, and started bowling fast.

That summer was one of the hottest in years and the pitches were harder and had more bounce. With the hook shot securely under my belt, I now returned bouncers to all those who had bombarded me during the previous season. To begin with, fast bowling was more a means of avenging myself than taking wickets. I often overdid the bouncer, sometimes bowling three or four an over, and developed something of a reputation on the county circuit. But the consistent use of the bouncer increased my pace as my body got stronger from the extra effort, and in the middle of the season Norman Gifford started giving me the new ball. My best performance was in the match against Lancashire: I made 111 not out and took 13 wickets. At the end of the season I was presented with the Weatherall Award for the best all-rounder. I had taken 65 wickets and averaged 40 with the bat. Among the Pakistanis playing county cricket that season, my batting average was only bettered by Zaheer Abbas. This was no mean achievement, since they included Sadiq and Mushtaq Mohammad, Asif Iqbal, Majid Khan and Intikhab Alam.

It came as something of a surprise when, on returning to Pakistan, I found that I had been relegated to number nine in the batting order for the first Test against New Zealand at Lahore. We were easily the better team and won the first two Tests with a day to spare. In this series I was given the new ball on a regular basis for the first time. I bowled my best spell in Test cricket to date in New Zealand's second innings at Lahore, taking four wickets.

Clean bowling Glenn Turner for one with a quick delivery was particularly satisfying. At Worcester he had said that I didn't have it in me to become a fast bowler. I also dismissed that other Worcestershire doubter, John Parker, four times out of six. Although I got my first Test fifty, my batting remained largely under wraps because of our powerful line-up. Basically an orthodox high-order batsman, I found it difficult to adjust to the requirements of batting lower down the order.

I left Worcester for a quite straightforward and, I feel, perfectly legitimate reason: I just didn't enjoy myself in the town. It is no disrespect to Worcester, but a reflection of my own way of life. I had no close friends: either the players were married and had their own lives, or they were unmarried and spent their evenings in pubs. Since I cannot stand pub life, being a teetotaller, I was lonely and bored. When I explained this to the club chairman, he could not understand my reasoning. He began by assuming that some club had offered me an enormous sum of money, after which he suddenly asked me if I was leaving because I couldn't find enough girls in the town. Later on, to my amusement, he made the same statement to the press. No wonder I was given a playboy image.

I have never since experienced the sense of excitement and anticipation that I felt before the 1976–7 tour of Australia and the West Indies. The senior players who had toured Australia in 1972–3 were unanimous in their admiration for Australian cricket – the competitive and aggressive attitude of the players, the excellent facilities, the knowledgeable and vociferous crowds, the hard, fast pitches. It was bound to be an exhilarating tour. We were going to take on easily the best team in the world in the best place to play cricket. For a young man eager to carve a name for himself, this was the ideal opportunity. The whole team, in fact, were anxious to prove themselves at the highest level.

We arrived in Australia to find that we were not rated very highly, and our first match in Perth seemed to confirm their low opinion of us: Western Australia needed 333 to win in four hours, and managed it with ease. Dennis Lillee claimed in his newspaper column that they would walk all over us. He thought we had a few good batsmen, and included me in this category, but as far as bowling was concerned he dismissed me as a medium-pace trundler who was not going to give anyone much trouble, and added that our seam bowling as a whole was not Test class.

At Adelaide we won the toss and batted first on a typical Australian pitch: with a little bounce it was excellent for stroke play. Lillee and Thomson, the duo which had destroyed England and the West Indies, soon had us in trouble. Then Thomson, trying to catch Zaheer off his own bowling, collided with Alan Turner and dislocated his shoulder, after which he was out of the match and the series. Zaheer went on to make 85, I contributed 48 and we reached 272. It was not much, considering the pitch and the depleted attack, but more than had seemed possible when we were 157 for 6.

The Australian innings confirmed everything that had been said about our seam bowling. Sarfraz, Salim Altaf and I were hammered all over the place. I took only one wicket for 92 runs, and still hadn't worked out how to bowl on Australian wickets. Bowling within the stumps was useless. The ball did not seam much and the Australians, superb on-side players, scored off me at will. Australia made 454 and the onus was now squarely on our top-order batsmen. They responded magnificently and we fought all the way down the order. Zaheer and Asif Iqbal hit hundreds, Asif playing the innings of the series. Coming in at 236 for 4, he took Pakistan to 466 and remained unbeaten with 152. Asif and Iqbal Qasim – who made 4 – added 87 runs for the tenth wicket.

With 285 to win, Australia were cruising at 200 for 3. The wicket was spinning a bit on the last day; Qasim, supported by Javed Miandad's leg-spin, had not let the Australian batsmen score quickly, and we had given nothing away in the field all day. When Qasim dismissed Greg Chappell he initiated a mini-collapse, and Australia required 56 runs off the last 15 overs, with four wickets in hand. Gary Cosier and Rodney Marsh chose to play out time and finished 24 runs short. The crowd felt that Australia had chickened out, and made plain their disapproval of their batting.

The press and the public now revised their opinion of our team, and the series was no longer seen as a walk-over. Our seam bowling, however, was still considered below par, and the second Test at Melbourne seemed to prove that their original assessment of the team in general and our pace bowling in particular had been accurate. Despite the overcast conditions, the Australians chose to bat. Sarfraz was unfit, and I shared the new ball with Salim Altaf. With the ball really swinging I just couldn't get it right. When I bowled fast I lost control, but if I tried to bowl line and length I failed to penetrate. After the Australian openers had put on 134 the cloud cover slowly lifted, and their batting made mincemeat of our attack. I could see that the team felt the seamers had really let them down. Australia declared at 517 for 8, and our batsmen reached 270 for 2 on what was now an easy-paced pitch. Then Lillee destroyed our middle order after taking the second new ball with one of the best spells of fast bowling I have ever seen. He finished with 6 for 82, and we were dismissed for 333.

In their second innings I decided that I was going to go flat out, whatever the consequences. I was fed up with being hit trying to concentrate on line and length. I managed to work up a good speed with an off-stump line. Some of the Australian batsmen were surprised: Marsh was late on a hook shot and got hit on the head. I took 5 for 122 in an Australian total of 315 for 8 declared. But in the second innings our batting collapsed and we lost the match by 348 runs, the heaviest defeat by a runs margin in our cricket history.

We went into the third Test at Sydney determined to show that we were not the rabbits the Australian press had once more decided us to be. Lillee, who had bowled us out on the easy-paced pitch at Melbourne, was visibly licking his lips at the prospect of bowling on the hard green Sydney wicket. He said as much, and to some extent succeeded in psyching us out. Mushtaq was certainly rattled, and we went into the match with only three specialist bowlers – two seamers and a spinner – and an extra batsman. This strange selection was typical of the defensive style of most Pakistani captains. The fear of losing had dominated Pakistan's cricket for so long that the tactic of packing the team with batsmen was an established practice.

Greg Chappell won the toss, and once again demonstrated his contempt for our fast bowling by choosing to bat in humid conditions on a well-grassed pitch. This time I got it right and, with Sarfraz, dismissed Australia cheaply. The run-up at Sydney suited me – it sloped gently towards the wicket, helping me to gain momentum without expending too much energy. The run-up had a lot to do with my rhythm at this stage. My action was not yet fluent enough and I needed a good approach for everything to click into place (even now, a good run-up helps me). At Sydney I was able to bowl fast and accurately for long spells. Australia made 211 in the first innings and I took 6 for 102.

Our batting also gave them a shock. We were supposed to roll over at the very sight of Dennis Lillee, and at 111 for 4 this seemed likely. Then Asif Iqbal, for the second time in the series, went into his 'into the valley of death' routine and made a remarkable hundred. This was the third such innings he had played for us in a matter of months. Haroon Rashid and Javed Miandad both got fifties, and helped Asif to take our score to 360. Haroon, in his Test debut, played a gritty and accomplished innings of 57 and stood up to Lillee at his fastest when Australia took the second new ball.

We had taken a sizeable lead and, for the first time in the series, the Australian batting was coming under pressure. I put everything into my bowling, and bowled unchanged for almost four hours – so much so that my shirt sleeve came off from the effort and the sweat. The Australian batting teetered and then collapsed to 99 for 7. Tail-end resistance from Marsh and Lillee saved them from an innings defeat, but we won by eight wickets on the fourth day. I took 6 for 63 in the second innings and had a match analysis of 12 for 165.

This was a turning point for me and for Pakistan cricket. We had achieved Pakistan's first Test victory in Australia and drawn the series. Suddenly we were a team to be reckoned with, and the shock waves of our victory reached the West

Indies, where people were anticipating a thrilling series.

As a result of the Sydney Test, some commentators had made rather exaggerated comments about my bowling prowess, saying that at times I bowled as fast as Lillee. When I arrived in the West Indies, Sir Garry Sobers took one look at me and said, 'If he's as quick as Lillee then Lillee must've been bowling at half pace!' Every West Indies club possesses a fast bowler, and they are not easily impressed. As I mentioned earlier, I could only bowl consistently fast when everything fell into place, and this didn't happen at all often in the West Indies. When we arrived we thought there would only be one fast bowler – Andy Roberts – to contend with, since Michael Holding was injured and was expected to miss the series. Little did we know. In a side game at St Lucia before the first Test we made the acquaintance of Messrs Croft and Garner. Both about six feet six inches tall, they were not only fast but generated a lot of bounce. They ran through our batting, and we lost the match. However, our confidence was not unduly shattered and we went into the first Test expecting it to be a tight match.

The first Test at Bridgetown was one of the finest I have ever played in. From start to finish it was completely unpredictable. We batted first and got off to a fine start, largely due to Majid, who was at his peak on this tour. Then Wasim Raja made an unbeaten 117 and, with the late-order batsmen, added 202 for the last four wickets. Throughout the tour our batting depended on Majid and Wasim Raja, who were the only players consistently able to get runs against the West Indies pace attack. The formidable West Indian batting line-up of Fredericks, Greenidge, Richards, Kallicharran and Lloyd tended to crack under pressure, and in the first Test Sarfraz and I had them in trouble at 183 for 5. The old ball was swinging and not coming on to the bat: Sarfraz had Lloyd and Deryck Murray tied down with controlled swing bowling. The new ball was due, and Mushtaq wanted to take it. Like most batsman-captains he had a rather simplistic, programmed approach in such situations. His own vulnerability to pace, after the going-over he had been given by Lillee in Australia, may have reinforced this batsman's-eye view of the new ball.

Sarfraz asked me to tell Mushtaq that the new ball would only give the batsmen a breathing space. A succession of Pakistani captains, including Mushtaq, couldn't take Sarfraz's unorthodox and unpredictable approach to the game and distrusted him. So I went up to Mushtaq and passed on Sarfraz's logic. But he would not listen. After all, if we were bowling so well with the old ball, what wonders might we not perform with a new one? It didn't work. The new ball came on to the bat, and on the bare pitch would neither swing nor seam. Lloyd opened his shoulders and knocked us all over the ground. He went on to make 157 and the West Indies reached 421 in reply to our total of 435. We collapsed to 153 for 9 against Roberts, Croft and Garner in the second innings. Then Wasim Raja and Wasim Bari had a gritty partnership; their luck held, and they put on 133 in 110 minutes for the tenth wicket. Needing 306 for victory, the West Indies were close to losing their first Test at Bridgetown since England beat them in 1934–5. They began confidently enough, but collapsed after Richards was dismissed for 92. After being reduced to 217 for 8, with fifteen minutes plus the last twenty overs to go, they batted out time. Roberts stayed at the wicket for ninety minutes, Holder for forty-five, and Croft batted through the final eight overs.

In the first innings of the second Test at Port-of-Spain, Colin Croft ran through our batting on a wet pitch, taking 8 for 29. We were dismissed for 180 and, with Sarfraz out of the team because of injury, it was up to me to engineer the fightback. Salim Altaf took two quick wickets, but I bowled appallingly: I lost my temper after being attacked by Fredericks and Greenidge, and became increasingly wild. We batted with greater purpose in the second innings and reached 340. By the time I got it all together for the first time on the tour, it was too late. The West Indies were 150 for 1, chasing 206, when I put in a spell of 3 for 10 – but then Wasim Bari dropped Kallichar-ran with the West Indies looking distinctly edgy, and it was all over. I was disappointed with my bowling on the tour thus far: except for that last spell it had lacked penetration.

The third Test at Georgetown typified Pakistan's batting performance at the time. In the first innings we were skittled out for 194. Then, after the West Indies had amassed a total of 448, our batting came good and put the match out of reach. In the second innings Majid made a brilliant 167. The entire top order supported him, and we batted for two days to save the match.

The fourth Test was played on a relatively slow pitch which took some spin. We batted first and made 341, Majid contributing 92 and Mushtaq 121. The West Indies declined from 73 for no wickets to 154 all out, and I bowled with pace and accuracy and movement, taking 4 for 64. The second innings followed a similar pattern. We topped 300 and the West Indies collapsed against Mushtaq's leg-spin and the swing of Sarfraz. The series was now tied, and everything depended on the final Test at Kingston, Jamaica.

The pitch at Sabina Park was unusually fast, with an uneven bounce. This was the wicket on which the West Indies had destroyed India the previous winter: three Indian batsmen had retired hurt and Bedi had closed India's second innings at 97 with two tail-enders yet to bat. There was no doubt that we would also receive our share of short-pitched bowling and would have to bat with great determination. At the end of a long and punishing tour our batting was showing signs of wear and tear, with only Majid and Wasim Raja displaying any kind of form. Sadiq Mohammad was not the same batsman after being hit on the jaw by Roberts in the third Test. Zaheer, who had played in only two Tests so far, was also shaky. Asif Iqbal hadn't sorted out Croft, while Mushtaq was visibly nervous against pace. Javed Miandad, still young and inexperienced, had been dropped after a string of failures in Australia and the West Indies. Despite the presence of seven specialist batsmen, the line-up didn't inspire much confidence. Before the match there was nervous talk about the pace and lift that Garner might extract from the pitch. At the same time the prospect of beating the West Indies on their own turf was exhilarating enough to stiffen our sinews. The mood on the eve of the final Test was a heady mixture of bravado and butterflies.

The West Indies batted first and were soon in trouble: 56 for 3 with Fredericks, Richards and Lloyd gone. In the intense, clammy heat I felt exhausted after only six overs. However, I had taken all three wickets and was enjoying the extra pace and bounce. There was still the small matter of Gordon Greenidge's wicket. He played one of the greatest Test innings I have seen: exactly 100 out of 280. Greenidge can be orthodox, but he can also be devastating. On that day he produced the best of both styles, mixing concentrated defence and furious assault. The moment he was gone the West Indies innings folded. I had taken 6 for 90 and was pretty pleased with my performance: 280 was not a large score on a small ground with an extremely fast outfield. We went in to bat forty minutes before the close on the first day, and before the day was over, 280 might as well have been 500. Andy Roberts bowled four extremely quick overs at Majid, and it was apparent that Majid was quite unnerved by this. The shock waves of those overs reverberated through the dressing-room. Majid had handled pace better than anyone else throughout the tour, both in Australia and the West Indies, and seeing him rattled had shaken our entire batting line-up.

I'll never forget the drive from the hotel to the ground the next morning. Hardly a word was spoken: we felt as though we were going to a funeral. Such experienced players should have realised that any fast bowler is capable of a spell in which everything clicks, in which the body is in complete harmony and achieves a perfect rhythm, enabling him to bowl extremely fast and dangerously; but that he cannot produce such spells at will. In the event, Roberts proved unable to bowl with the same pace and fire that day. But the damage had been done. Our batsmen were living in fear, and got themselves out to wild shots. We were 122 for 5 when Wasim Raja joined Haroon Rashid, who was batting sensibly and well. The leg-spinner Holford was bowling: Wasim jumped down the pitch and was lucky not to be stumped. Then he hit Holford for six, and a few deliveries later holed out trying to repeat the shot. Wasim had scored over 400 runs in the first four Tests, and this strange exhibition can only be understood in the context of Roberts's spell. Asif committed suicide in a similar fashion. Only Haroon, our most recent entrant into Test cricket, took on the West Indian pace bowlers. I can still remember two magnificent sixes over mid-wicket off Garner. For much of Haroon's innings I was at the other end, admiring his skill and courage.

We were dismissed for 198, and might well have been more than 82 runs behind after such a spineless batting perform-ance. Unfortunately, Wasim Bari, our wicket-keeper, had retired hurt after being hit in the face trying to hook Croft. Majid kept wicket, and dropped Greenidge early in the second innings. The West Indian openers eventually put on 183 for the first wicket, as much due to our dejected bowling attack as their good batting. A spineless display of batting often de-moralises the team's bowling attack. By the end of the third day we realised that we would have to make something close to 400 to win the match. Because the series was tied, the final Test was being played over seven days – including the rest day – in order to produce a result. On the rest day (the fourth day) it became clear that the team had already surrendered. We were booked to fly back to Pakistan on the evening of the final day, but the players were so anxious to leave that new bookings were made for the evening of the penultimate day – an astonishing admission of a general lack of resolve. Mushtaq was so obviously afraid of fast bowling that he was hardly in a position to rally the team – nor did he try to. In fact he made matters more difficult for himself by questioning the bowling actions of Roberts and Garner in a pre-match interview – not the smartest way of appeasing his tormentors.

Set 442 to win, we were soon 51 for 4. Asif Iqbal then played an innings that at least partly salvaged our reputation, if not our self-respect. He put on a dazzling exhibition of stroke play and notched up another incredible century. During a partnership of 115 for the sixth wicket with Wasim Raja he protected him from Andy Roberts. Watching from the dressing-room we were puzzled when they refused some easy singles to third man and fine leg, and Wasim later admitted he had told Asif that it would be better for the team if Asif took on Roberts while he handled the rest of the attack.

When I went in to join Asif I knew I was in for some rough treatment. Roberts and I had exchanged bouncers throughout the series. The crowd, sensing what was coming, chanted 'Blood, blood'. Roberts was in the middle of his second really quick spell of the match. Needless to say I knew that not many deliveries were going to be pitched up, so I was ready on the back foot almost before the ball was delivered. The first two balls hit my gloves before I was halfway through the hook shot. The next one was pitched up and I got a couple of runs. The fourth was one of the fastest deliveries I have ever faced. Before I could notice anything it had kissed my cap, just touched Deryck Murray's gloves and gone for byes. An inch closer and it would probably have ended my career. After this experience I had no hesitation in donning a helmet the moment they came into use. I went on to make 22: we totalled 301 and lost the match by 140 runs.

Despite the fiasco of the final Test it had been a close and absorbing series. My only regret is that I didn't play another Test series in the West Indies until 1988. During the tour, Tony Greig had come to the West Indies on behalf of Kerry Packer to recruit players for a World XI that would play a series against the Australian team in the coming winter. The World XI would be chosen from a squad of fourteen players – four South Africans, four West Indians, three Englishmen and three Pakistanis (Asif, Majid and myself). I was thrilled to be included in the squad. Only a year earlier I had been unsure of my place in the Pakistan side, yet I would soon be playing with the world's best in Australia, a magnificent place to play cricket, for a lot of money. As far as my Test career was concerned, I would only miss one series – England's tour of Pakistan in the winter of 1977–8. Or so I thought.

CHAPTER 3

All over the Place

It's possible that some of the Australian players may have realised that the first Packer series could lead to a serious rift in the cricketing world, but I don't think any of the West Indian, Pakistani or English players harboured such suspicions. With hindsight, this seems extremely naive – after all, the Australian Board was unlikely to take a parallel series lying down. Most of us assumed that some agreement would be reached that would include Kerry Packer's 'Australia versus a World XI' project. Little did we know that all hell was about to break loose. The Australian Board banned their players who had signed with Packer, and put pressure on the ICC to have the rest of us banned. Although it was not their problem, the Pakistani and English Boards fell into line. Those countries whose players had not been invited by Packer – India and New Zealand – joined the shrill chorus of denunciation. Only the West Indian controlling body approached the matter sensibly.

The moment the battle lines had been drawn up, Kerry Packer signed the whole West Indian team as well as additional English and Pakistani players (Mushtaq and Zaheer). The reaction to our signing with Kerry Packer was so extreme and so ludicrous that the players closed ranks and were determined to stick it out, even if it meant forgoing their Test careers for a while. We embarked on a couple of seasons of Packer cricket with some misgivings, but a good deal of excitement at the prospect of playing with and against the best players in the world, for Packer cricket was to be the toughest test of skill and stamina I have ever experienced. On the other hand, it lacked the tension of Test matches and the adrenalin that flows when one plays for one's country. Beyond a certain point it is difficult to bowl to brilliant batsmen or face a battery of fast bowlers day after day simply in order to prove one's individual worth.

Packer cricket was so unremittingly difficult that some batsmen were permanently scarred by the experience. All three teams – Australia, the West Indies and the World XI – had such ferocious pace attacks that there was never any relief. Despite the introduction of helmets – which were absolutely essential – batting was a hazardous business. There were no minor games in which a batsman could recuperate. A few reputations were made, but more were punctured. Vivian Richards stood out: one could see that he was in a different class from the Chappell brothers, Barry Richards, Majid and Greenidge, all of whom were great players but really in the second rank compared to Viv at the time. Of the Pakistani batsmen, Mushtaq, already suspect against pace, vanished into oblivion. Majid, who had stopped playing for Glamorgan, and had taken seven months off from cricket, was not prepared for the calibre of bowling he had to face, and it took him some time to adjust: he was never quite the batsman he should have been. Zaheer did not make an impact until the second year. Surprisingly, Asif Iqbal proved to be not only the best Pakistani batsman but also one of the most successful middle-order batsmen of the Packer years. Some reputations were damaged beyond repair, particularly Tony Greig's. His bowling was largely innocuous and his batting technique was exposed by the barrage of short-pitched bowling. Ironically, one of the main organisers of Packer cricket was quite unsuited to meet its special demands.

As far as I was concerned, the Packer years were largely beneficial. I had the chance to learn from watching the world's finest fast bowlers. Mike Procter and John Snow taught me a lot: Snow emphasised the necessity of getting side-on and closer to the stumps, while Procter helped me with my run-up, which was still that of a medium-pacer, short and mincing.

31

This put a strain on me and destroyed my rhythm. After a lot of hard work, I got it right – a smooth, natural approach culminating in a jump that helped me to get side-on. I also learned how to use the entire width of the bowling crease. By the end of the Packer era I could produce spells of accurate and hostile fast bowling with some regularity.

This was also the period in which my 'star' status was established. Packer's organisation chose to promote individuals in a way that had never been attempted before. They did their bit, and I did mine by performing on the field. Since then the media hype has hardly stopped, for good and for bad. All the publicity over the years had primarily to do with being a successful cricketer: the rest was incidental as far as I was concerned.

Packer cricket was responsible for many major developments in the sport. The improvement of protective gear was a direct result of the unusual number of fast bowlers in World Series Cricket. Injuries were frequent, and the batsman urgently needed better protection. The number of one-day internationals also went up dramatically. The original idea was to stage 'Super Tests', but public interest and the players' enthusiasm for this form of cricket could not be sustained in the absence of official 'Test' status. Ian Chappell was largely responsible for keeping the team motivated for the five-day game. It soon became apparent that the one-day format attracted larger crowds and this led not only to an increase in the number of one-day matches but also to the introduction of night cricket, together with coloured clothing and a white ball. Night cricket attracted an entirely new type of spectator to the game. The conservatives in our midst had their reservations, but the rest of us, who thought we were part of a revolution, wanted to try it out.

Another feature of Packer cricket was the personalisation and marketing of players so as to appeal to live and television spectators. In the absence of patriotic passions the game was promoted by emphasising its entertainment value and by glamorising the players, largely through outstanding television coverage. Up to nine cameras were employed to give multi-angled replays and close-ups. Before the first night match at Sydney the players and organisers sat around, waiting to see what kind of response this strange scheme would get. It succeeded beyond anyone's wildest imagination. The ground was sold out, and the spectactor response was fantastic.

World Series Cricket was responsible for bringing the game into line with the commercial demands of modern sport. Players' salaries rose dramatically – not just for Test players, but for other first-class cricketers as well. The game also generated more income, as sponsors and advertisers became conscious of its market value. And the influx of money and glamour made it more likely that talented young players would want to make a career out of cricket. Such sweeping changes inevitably had their drawbacks. Commercialisation undermined certain aspects of the game; but this was probably inevitable, and World Series Cricket only hastened the process. Of more immediate relevance was the ill-feeling that pervaded the game for two years and the devaluation of Test cricket in this period as a result of the banning of the Packer players.

I was surprised by the intense hostility most county cricketers showed towards the Packerites. At a special Cricketers' Association meeting in England, 60 per cent of the members wanted Packer players to be banned from county cricket. Even worse, a majority supported a motion demanding the expulsion of all overseas players from county cricket as well. This meeting was a real eye-opener, and I resigned my membership of the Association on the spot. I found its position untenable and hypocritical, for it had taken no such stand over the issue of apartheid: in fact, the Association supported players who chose to supplement their income by going to South Africa. Obviously no moral principles were involved in the Association's stand against the Packer players – it seemed to be much more a question of jealousy. For example, Bob Willis turned very anti-Packer, yet he had been on the verge of signing for Packer and only decided against because he discovered that by staying in Test cricket he could make more money. And yet for all the excitement of World Series Cricket, I really missed the tension and commitment of proper Test cricket. Had WSC gone on for another season, as originally planned, I think a number of players – including me – would have dropped out.

In December 1977 we were informed by Omar Kureishi, a prominent Pakistani journalist and former administrator, that the BCCP wanted us to play in the home series against England. Pleased at this change of heart, Kerry Packer agreed to release us temporarily and even paid part of our travelling expenses. Delighted at the prospect of playing for Pakistan again, Mushtaq, Zaheer and I flew home. Meanwhile, the English team had categorically refused to play if we were included. On our arrival in Karachi we found that we were an unwanted and embarrassing presence for the Board, which was split itself and which had succumbed to the threat of a boycott and reneged on their decision to play us. The BCCP refused to acknowledge that we had been summoned. Even our own players gave us the cold shoulder, and in the end we repacked our bags and flew back to Australia.

That summer, 1978, England destroyed what was virtually a Pakistani second team. I was then playing county cricket for Sussex and felt quite depressed watching the series on television. But at least the series revealed the inadequacy of the team without the Packer players. Later that year, the Indian team was due to visit Pakistan, a resumption of cricketing relations after nearly eighteen years. It soon became obvious that Pakistani public opinion would not tolerate a series against the old enemy in which all our best players were missing. A new Board, under General Azhar, was formed by General Zia, and our ban was lifted. Most of us were playing county cricket when we learned that before long we would not only be playing Test cricket again, but in an historic series against India. I was keen to be at my fittest for this encounter. I had torn a muscle towards the end of the county season, so I had to do all I could to get fit in time for the first Test.

Opposite: 1. The first Test against the West Indies at Lahore, 1980

2, 3, 4. My first Test century at
Lahore, 1980, after which I
was made Man of the Match.
Above Clive Lloyd is at short
leg while *opposite* Joel Garner
is the bowler. *Left*
Congratulations from
my team-mates during
a bowling spell

When we arrived back in Pakistan the excitement in the country was incredible. The media were full of analyses of and comments about the approaching series. There was a general feeling of optimism about the chances of Pakistan winning its first rubber against India. The strength of the Indian side at that time lay in the spin bowling of Bedi, Chandrasekhar and Prasanna. When we arrived at Faisalabad for the first Test, Sarfraz and I were amazed when we saw the pitch. There was not a blade of grass on it and it shone like a mirror. India did not have any pace bowling to speak of – Kapil Dev, who made his debut in this Test, was still an unknown quantity. When we enquired about the state of the wicket we learnt that the groundsman had been instructed not to provide any kind of surface that the Indian spinners could possibly use. Despite our clear advantage in pace bowling, the fear of losing overrode any attempt to win.

The wicket was a batsman's paradise. We batted first and made 503 for 8, with Zaheer and Javed Miandad both scoring big hundreds. The Indians in their turn were not to be denied and also made an extremely large score. Mushtaq's post-match comments were quite amazing. He blamed Sarfraz and me for bowling too short, not realising that on such a dead wicket it was the only way to try to contain the batsmen and force them into error.

Pakistan's cricket establishment, helped by some goading from senior players, summoned up a bit of courage and prepared a green wicket for the second Test in Lahore. This match was played in late October, and we knew that whatever life there was in the Gaddafi Stadium pitch would not last long in the heat. Luckily for us, Mushtaq won the toss and put India in to bat. The onus was now squarely on our shoulders. I got two early wickets and Salim Altaf accounted for Gavaskar. Then Sarfraz bowled magnificently, and we got India out for less than 200. Sarfraz and I took four wickets apiece. We put up a huge total, entirely due to a splendid double-century by Zaheer Abbas, who showed why he was known as the king of spin: a complete master of spin bowling, he treated the Indian

Opposite: 5. Third Test at Melbourne, 1981

spinners with disdain on a pitch that didn't help them much either.

By now the wicket had eased up, and we knew that it wouldn't be easy to dismiss India for a second time. The Indian openers, Gavaskar and Chetan Chauhan, played sensible cricket and put on 192 before we got our first wicket. With only a day left, it seemed that India would save the match, and they were well on their way to doing so when Mudassar initiated a mid-innings collapse. We were left needing 126 for victory in approximately 100 minutes, and reached our target with eight overs to spare.

There was jubilation throughout the country, and the government even proclaimed the next day a national holiday. We were now one up, with one match to play. Two pitches were prepared in Karachi – a green one and a brown batting one. Amazingly, Mushtaq opted for the dead one to protect our lead. However, in spite of the wicket, the match developed quite differently. The atmosphere at Karachi always provides a bit of movement for swing bowlers, and Sarfraz and I were able to work through India's batting line-up, until they were all out for 344. When we came in to bat, our middle and late order took us from 198 for 5 to 481 for 9 declared. Javed made exactly 100, and all the tail-end batsmen contributed useful runs. India's second innings followed the pattern of their first: they had a middle-order collapse, but were steadied by resolute batting by Gavaskar, who made his second century of the match. But our pace attack steadily chipped away at their batting and, as at Lahore, we dismissed them late on the fifth day, only to be left facing an even more difficult target. An exciting run chase followed – I was promoted to number four in the batting order, hitting Bedi for two sixes and a four in an over – and we reached our target with just seven balls to spare. We had beaten the Indians 2-0, and the country was ecstatic.

Not even in our wildest dreams could we have imagined a more triumphant homecoming. The abuse the Packer players had faced over the past two years was suddenly a distant memory; we were all heroes. The series against India sparked off a cricket boom in Pakistan which has lasted till the present day. The Pakistani public had been brought up on a diet of slow, tedious, negative cricket played on dead pitches, a foolproof recipe for an interminable succession of drawn matches. The victory over India, with the exciting run chases at Lahore and Karachi, was a novel experience for our cricket fans. Television coverage of Test matches was also very new, and for the first time people in small towns, and even in some villages, became part of Pakistan's cricket-watching population. Cricket fever reached an incredible pitch, a level of excitement that was only repeated during the 1987 World Cup.

Although we had beaten India comprehensively, I didn't share the general belief that Pakistan had a formidable batting line-up. On the evidence of the Indian series it certainly seemed that way, but I had seen our batsmen play a different class of bowling in Packer cricket and knew their limitations. However, in the general euphoria of our victory over India, nobody was in the mood for a rational assessment of our strengths and weaknesses.

At the end of the series, the Packer players all left for Australia and rejoined World Series Cricket. The rest of the team, under Mushtaq, flew to New Zealand, where we were supposed to meet up with them once our season's commitment to Packer was over. By the time we arrived in New Zealand, Pakistan were already one up in the series with two to play. In the first Test at Christchurch Javed Miandad had batted extremely well in both innings, while Mushtaq and Wasim Raja had spun out New Zealand with their leg-spinners in the fourth innings.

The rest of the series was rather boring and inconsequential. The second Test at Napier was a high-scoring draw, but the third and final match at Auckland was interesting for a while. New Zealand batted first, and at one stage Sarfraz and I had reduced them to 60 for 5 before Jeremy Coney and the tail took their score to 254. We made 359 in reply, with Zaheer Abbas scoring a chancy 135. New Zealand went in to bat 105 runs behind, and although I felt their second innings saw one of my better spells in Test cricket, I managed only two wickets. I beat the batsmen on numerous occasions and we would have won but for dropped catches and some rather dubious umpiring decisions.

We left for Australia in March 1979 to play a short end-of-season series consisting of just two Tests. They were played in as ugly an atmosphere as I've known in my career. This was the first time Packer players had played against non-Packer players in Australia. The media played up this aspect of the series, and the comments of some of the players only served to sour the relationship between the two teams. Asif Iqbal made an extremely ill-judged remark before the series began, saying that the Australian team was sub-standard, and that we were going to play against a bunch of schoolboys. The Australian players, who had just been thrashed 5-1 by England and were desperate to prove them-selves, didn't take kindly to such remarks and retaliated. At the first Test in Melbourne we won the toss and chose to bat first – and our vaunted batting line-up was bundled out for 196 by Rodney Hogg and Alan Hurst. My misgivings about our batting order were only strengthened by this dismal perform-ance. Luckily, Australia in their turn could only make 168. The bad feeling between the two sides was deepened by an unfortunate and unnecessary incident.

Javed Miandad ran out Rodney Hogg after the batsman had gone down to inspect the pitch. I thought it was very funny, because Javed was brought up in the type of highly competitive street cricket in which this sort of thing was commonplace – every rule in the book was stretched to get people out. Fielders would tell a batsman that he had dropped something on the pitch, and when he went to retrieve it they'd run him out. The moment Hogg went down the pitch, with the ball still in play, I expected something like this might happen. Mushtaq asked the umpire to revoke his decision but his request was denied. Hogg smashed his stumps before leaving. 'I was surprised that he left one stump standing,' his captain later commented.

We made 353 for 9 in our second innings, with Majid contributing a century in typical style. Australia were left needing 382 to win, and we felt sure that their batting was not strong enough to reach such a target. However, Allan Border and Kim Hughes shared a sensible partnership which took Australia to the verge of victory; at one stage, with seven wickets in hand, they needed only 76 runs to win, which seemed a mere formality. Then Sarfraz Nawaz bowled Border, and the Australian batting simply folded up. Five runs later they were all out, having collapsed from 305 for 3 to 310 all out. Sarfraz produced what must rank as one of the great spells of bowling in Test cricket, taking the last seven wickets for one run in just 33 deliveries. He finished with an analysis of 9 for 86, the other batsman being run out. This inspirational spell was typical of Sarfraz, an intelligent and experienced bowler who knew how to make the most of the conditions. He always seemed to know which ball would swing more than others and, as a result, he invariably made the choice when the umpires presented a box of new balls.

We went into the second and last Test at Perth in a thoroughly negative state of mind after our captain, Mushtaq, had told us during a team meeting that we should make sure we drew the match. I've always been against this type of thinking, because it is usually a recipe for disaster if a team approaches a match with the specific intention of drawing it. Mushtaq packed the team with batsmen and we went into the match with only three front-line bowlers. Sarfraz and I had both been playing non-stop cricket for many months now and were showing signs of wear and tear. I had a back strain which had to be treated during the intervals to keep me going. Sikander Bakht pulled a muscle and could only bowl 10.5 overs in the match, which left Sarfraz and me to do the bulk of the bowling.

We batted first and, apart from Javed Miandad, who made 129, none of the other batsmen made many runs and we were dismissed for a meagre score of 277. Against what was virtually a two-man bowling attack, Australia had little trouble in taking a lead of 50. In the second innings our batsmen once again failed under pressure, and only a fighting century by Asif Iqbal kept us in the game. Asif and Sikander Bakht were putting up stubborn resistance for the last wicket when Hurst ran out Sikander as he was backing up. Asif then smashed the stumps, just as Hogg had in Melbourne. We were thoroughly incensed by this, and decided that we would retaliate as soon as an opportunity presented itself. Australia were 87 for no wickets and well on their way to victory when Andrew Hilditch retrieved a wayward return and handed the ball to the bowler, Sarfraz; Sarfraz appealed, and Hilditch was given out for handling the ball. Australia then proceeded to win the match quite easily by seven wickets.

This series left an unpleasant taste in the mouth, and a big question mark over the strength of our team. We had managed to draw the series only by the skin of our teeth against an inexperienced Australian side that was missing most of its top players. It was an ill-conceived, ill-judged series which the Australian Board had arranged simply to deny Packer any further chance of televised cricket, and we should never have played it. By the end of the series the Australian press and the crowds were extremely hostile to us as a result of the ugly incidents on the field.

The defeat at Perth also signalled the end of Mushtaq Mohammad's captaincy. He was no longer certain of his place in the team: as a batsman he was now thoroughly suspect against pace bowling, and he was basically playing as a leg-spinner. As his batting deteriorated he had become increasingly defensive and nervous as the captain.

Asif Iqbal, who was batting better than ever, was appointed the new captain for the 1979 World Cup and the subsequent tour of India. The era of 'superstars' – the Packer players – was coming to an end, as most of them had passed their peak. But because of the poor standard of Pakistan's domestic cricket, new talent was not available.

Pakistan's performance in the 1979 World Cup emphasised our decline as well as the team's collective inability to cope with tension. We lost our group match with England after restricting them to 165 in 60 overs. Our batting capitulated against excellent bowling by Mike Hendrick, and at one stage we were 34 for 6. Despite this pathetic performance by our top order we lost the match by only 15 runs, and had to play the West Indies in the semi-finals. We gave them quite a fight on a feather-bed pitch at The Oval. They put up a huge total of 293 for 6, but the wicket was so slow that not even the West Indian pace quartet could get anything out of it, and at one stage we were 176 for 1, with Majid and Zaheer playing brilliantly. By now the West Indies bowling was looking quite ragged and they were patently nervous. After Zaheer's dismissal, I felt that Asif should have changed the batting order and not sent in Haroon Rashid, who lacked sufficient experience of one-day cricket and got bogged down. Haroon wasted valuable overs and put unnecessary pressure on the rest of the batting, and our senior batsmen got out trying to force the pace.

In 1978 Pakistan and India had resumed cricketing relations after some eighteen years. It had taken that long to overcome the hostility engendered by two wars between the countries. Sporting encounters between Pakistan and India have always generated high passions: even now, in one-day cricket, winning against each other is considered more important than eventual success in the competition. Sporting encounters strain the fragile relationship between Muslim and Hindu in India: people die of heart attacks during Tests and ten-year-old boys have stabbed each other during heated arguments about cricket matches.

The Indian team was comprehensively beaten on its tour of Pakistan in 1978—9. When we returned to India the following year, we were clear favourites: even Gavaskar, then India's captain, issued a statement saying that we would win easily. India's great spinners, Bedi, Chandrasekhar and Prasanna, had retired, while Venkataraghavan was out of form and favour: India's bowling attack of Kapil Dev, Ghavri, Binny, Doshi and Yadav didn't seem to pose much of a threat to our array of stroke-makers.

But we were over-confident. Mistakes had been made in

selection: Sarfraz was omitted because Asif Iqbal, our new captain, felt he could not handle him, and Mushtaq, the only survivor from the previous tour of India, was left out, as he was considered suspect against high pace. Although this was true, he would not have been in trouble against India's limited pace attack.

None of the players had any notion of the pressures of an Indian tour. From the moment we arrived it seemed as though the entire country had become a huge spotlight, trained solely on us. The relentless publicity, the huge partisan crowds in the jam-packed stadiums, the expectations of our own public – all these were too much for some of our players. Our batting, never famous for its resilience, went to pieces. Zaheer, always highly strung, was the first to crack. The previous year he had scored 583 runs, averaging 194.33, in the three Tests against India. This time he averaged 19, and seemed visibly relieved when he was dropped for the final Test. Majid looked shaky, and averaged only 20 despite being dropped down the order in the later matches. Mudassar, our other opener, hit a century in the first Test but never passed 30 after that. After the first Test we never reached 300 in any innings. Only Wasim Raja, and to some extent Javed Miandad, emerged with any credit from the tour.

Despite the fact that our batting flopped we should have drawn, or even won, the series. The wicket for the second Test at Delhi helped the seamers, but I was hampered by a rib-muscle injury and bowled only 8.3 overs. Sikander Bakht bowled his heart out and took 11 wickets: but it was not enough, and India were able to bat out the last day and a half.

After this Test it was suggested that Sarfraz should be called in reinforce the team, but Asif refused even to consider the proposal. I was therefore under great pressure to play in the third Test, which I did: the rib muscle went again in my first over, and I was in acute pain afterwards. I did dismiss Chauhan, after which Iqbal Qasim and Sikander reduced India to 154 for 6, but I was unable to come back, and the tail-enders added 180. Neither side topped 200 in the other innings, and India won on the fourth day.

Knowing I would definitely miss the fourth Test at Kanpur, India produced a well-grassed pitch, supposedly to assist Kapil Dev. They batted, and struggled to 162 against our back-up seamers, Sikander and Ehteshamuddin. We replied with 249, thanks almost entirely to Wasim Raja's brilliant 94 not out, and were in a useful position before rain, which penetrated the covers, washed out the final day's play.

Although I was still not fully fit I felt I had to play in the fifth Test, but it was apparent that our team had given up. They were thoroughly despondent − there was an atmosphere of despair in the dressing-room, and when we batted some players were too nervous to watch. On a perfect batting pitch we were dismissed for 272, with a number of batsmen reaching 30 but none of them having the patience or the will to stick it out. Zaheer, who was convinced that someone had put a spell on him, made a duck. When India batted, Gavaskar, a master of attrition, made 166 in almost ten hours, and set up the match for his side. I took five wickets, not a bad effort as my injury was still very painful. Our second-innings batting display was even worse, and India won easily by 10 wickets.

By the last Test I was fully fit and took nine wickets. I thought that we had a chance to salvage some self-respect before going home, but there was to be no fairy-tale ending. We dropped a number of catches and let India off the hook: they took the series 2-0.

All of us dreaded returning home, and we were right. No Pakistani team has ever had to face such humiliation, collectively and individually. Our failure was attributed to non-stop partying and a thoroughly irresponsible way of life. Apparently we had all indulged in wining, dining and womanising throughout the tour. There was little sympathy for my muscle injury, which I had evidently contracted while performing debauched calisthenics with Indian actresses.

Realistically, it should have been pointed out that our batting had always tended to collapse under pressure, but in the context of an India-Pakistan series rational analysis is rare indeed. The press thrives on innuendo, gossip, rumour and outright slander, and still more so at the first sign of defeat. My biggest crime was to have been outperformed by India's star all-rounder, Kapil Dev.

Foreseeing these recriminations, Asif Iqbal announced his retirement before we arrived home. During the tour he was a shadow of his former self. He was on tranquillisers and, already a wiry man, he lost a lot of weight. It was not until 1986–7, when I toured India as captain and lost half a stone, that I understood the pressures he must have been under.

It was this story of dishonour and disgrace that was primarily responsible for my continuing to bowl through the 1982–3 series against India with a leg fracture. The desire to erase the bad memories of that tour by comprehensively beating the old enemy was too strong. Since then I have realised that such passions are out of place on the cricket field, and can only do harm: but it is difficult to be objective when one's country's hopes and one's self-respect are riding on the result of a series.

After our return from India, Asif retired, the entire Board was changed, and there was widespread disenchantment with the senior players. The new president of the Board, Air Marshal Nur Khan, decided that it was time to make sweeping changes and appointed Javed Miandad captain over the heads of at least six players. This was a major error which led to immediate problems, since Javed was too young to handle the team and it was unfair on him to make him captain. Zaheer in particular felt hard done by: as the senior player, he thought he should have been the new captain.

Australia toured Pakistan early in 1980 and the cracks in the team were temporarily papered over by the old method of preparing slow pitches. We won the first Test at Karachi on a slow turning wicket, then proceeded to draw the other two on pitches that were so placid that it was difficult to complete an innings. The nature of the pitches was reflected in Dennis Lillee's performance. In three Tests he could only take three wickets, and conceded over 300 runs. At Faisalabad even

Taslim Arif, the wicket-keeper, made a double-century against him. The familiar scoreline of 'caught Marsh, bowled Lillee' was nowhere in evidence throughout the series. However, the series against Australia proved nothing about our abilities, while Javed made the atmosphere within the team more tense by dropping Zaheer for the third Test at Lahore.

The following winter the West Indies toured Pakistan, and the same strategy was adopted. But despite the slow, under-prepared pitches, the West Indian pace battery of Marshall, Garner, Croft and Clarke proved too much to handle. In the first Test at Lahore, on a perfect wicket, we collapsed to 95 for 5. Batting at number seven, I recorded my first Test century on my twenty-eighth birthday, so enabling us to reach 369, and from that point on the match headed towards an inevitable draw.

The next Test at Faisalabad was played on a spinning wicket and everything seemed to be in our favour. But once again our batting revealed our complete inability to handle sustained pace bowling. Zaheer, who had missed the first Test on the pretext of a shoulder injury, looked thoroughly suspect against pace and was in a terrible state against Marshall and Clarke, actually backing away from the fast bowling. I knew that this was the beginning of the end for Zaheer's reputation, because once a batsman is known to be afraid of pace he is in real trouble, and very rarely comes back – and every pace bowler then pitches short to him.

The first day and a half of the third Test at Karachi was washed out. Then Javed Miandad made the peculiar decision to bat first on a wicket that was still damp, and we were blasted out for 128. The match did nothing for Zaheer's confidence, after a Clarke bouncer had left a dent in his helmet. The West Indies did not fare much better, however, and Iqbal Qasim and I dismissed them for 169. We went into this Test with only one seam bowler – myself. I found myself tiring very quickly, because with a spinner operating at the other end I did not get much time to recuperate between overs. Because of the loss of play due to rain, the match was drawn.

In the last Test match at Multan – which was also drawn because of rain – I produced my best bowling of the series, taking 5 for 62 in the West Indies' first innings. Vivian Richards played a superb innings for them, making 120 out of 249, and holding the innings together in his own inimitable fashion. The story of our first innings was a repetition of the previous matches. It made no difference how slow we made the pitches, and we couldn't even reach 200.

By the end of this series, our batting was in tatters. We had no opening pair to speak of, Zaheer was a shadow of his former self, and Majid was no longer the batsman he had been. Javed and Wasim Raja performed reasonably, but nobody really stood out. It was obvious that we were going to have a tough time on the tour of Australia that winter.

I approached the Australian tour with mixed feelings. I was looking forward to bowling on pitches that would help me for the first time in almost two years of Test cricket. On the other hand, the state of the team was depressing, to say the least. There was no team spirit, and much ill-feeling in the dressing-room. It was clear that disaster lay ahead.

For a batting side that was so suspect against pace bowling, the fast wicket at Perth was the worst place in which to open a Test series. The match began well for us, and our seam attack dismissed Australia for only 180. As I'd expected, I was enjoying my bowling and took four wickets. But when we came in to bat all our worst fears were realised, and in no time at all we were 26 for 8 against the bowling of Dennis Lillee and Terry Alderman. Eventually we were bowled out for 62, losing the match by a huge margin of 262 runs. The match was notable for a childish incident between Javed Miandad and Lillee.

Our hitherto slow decline was now proceeding at breakneck speed, so much so that we looked like a second-rate team. Mohsin Khan was flown out to strengthen our batting, and immediately looked far more capable of handling pace than most of the team. But this belated infusion could not stop the rot. We were easily beaten once again, by 10 wickets, in the second Test at Brisbane. On a pitch that did not have that much pace in it, our batting failed to reach 300, yet Greg Chappell demonstrated how a batsman could pile up the runs on such a wicket, and his double-century was a cool, efficient innings that enabled Australia to declare at 512 for 9. Our second innings was, if anything, an even more pathetic display of batting. The wicket was not doing very much, and we only had to bat out the last day to save the game. Mudassar and Mohsin got us off to a good start, putting on 72 for the first wicket, but the rest of our batting couldn't last out the four hours that were left.

On a slower, spinning pitch at Melbourne we beat Australia by an innings in the third and final Test. This was the kind of wicket we were used to playing on in Pakistan, and our batting finally clicked. Although in the end we lost the series only 2-1, this failed to give a true picture of events. We had been shown up as a team of limited resources under conditions that did not favour us. Although I had taken 16 wickets in the three Tests, made a few runs and was the man of the series, I was not that pleased with myself. It had been a very unhappy tour, and by the end of it most of the players felt thoroughly disgusted. Things got so bad that there was an open and abusive confrontation between Javed and Zaheer in the dressing-room.

The Board reappointed Javed Miandad as captain for the Sri Lankan tour of Pakistan, beginning in March 1982. By this time, most of the players had serious reservations about his captaincy, but would have probably accepted the Board's decision had it not issued a statement implying that senior players were disloyal. The players believed that Javed had told the Board that the reason for our disastrous performance was the non-cooperation of senior players. We were furious, and certainly not prepared to take such a slur lying down. The entire team issued a counter-statement in which we rejected this view and said that we were no longer willing to play under Javed. The Board refused to back down and replied by picking an entirely new Test side. A few of the players left our ranks after they had been threatened with the loss of their jobs. Nevertheless, the Pakistani team that played against Sri Lanka in the first two Tests was really a second eleven team.

Pakistan won the first Test rather easily, but were then very lucky not to be beaten in the second match at Faisalabad. After the second Test, the Sri Lankans virtually accused our umpires of cheating to help the home team save the match. Our team's display in this match weakened the Board's position, and they knew that they would be in real trouble if Pakistan performed as badly in the final Test at Lahore. Javed was gently persuaded to resign from the captaincy as soon as the Sri Lankan Tests were over, and once he had issued a statement to this effect the dispute was resolved, and Pakistan once again had a full-strength side for the last Test. We beat Sri Lanka by an innings at Lahore. I bowled one of my better spells in Test cricket, taking 14 wickets in the match. I suppose that by not playing in the first two Test matches against the Sri Lankans, I may have lost an opportunity for taking a number of wickets which would have helped the final record, but the performances that have given me real satisfaction have always been against top teams.

Before our tour of England in the summer of 1982 there was much speculation about who was going to be the next captain. Matters became rather complicated when Javed and Zaheer both made it known that they would not play under each other. It was generally assumed that Javed would be nominated, but at the time there was a question mark over his place in the side; and this prompted the Board, much to my surprise, to ring me up in England and ask whether I would be interested in taking the job.

CHAPTER 4

Captain of Pakistan

It hadn't crossed my mind that I would ever be asked to captain Pakistan, nor had it been one of my ambitions. Ambition has always played an important part in my life: to begin with I had wanted to be selected for Pakistan as a batsman or a bowler, and then, when I seemed to be making progress as an all-rounder, I wanted to be recognised as the best all-rounder in Pakistan, and finally as the best all-rounder in the world. But the idea of being captain did not interest me particularly: I never thought it would happen, because for some reason fast bowlers have always been considered unsuitable for the job.

When I discussed the captaincy with friends I became discouraged. My close friend Iftikhar Ahmed, who has been a well-known commentator on cricket in Pakistan for many years, tried to dissuade me from accepting the job, because he felt that the extra pressures of captaincy could adversely affect an all-rounder's performance. He gave me the example of Ian Botham, who only the previous year had been removed from the captaincy of England after a disastrous spell: it may have been a coincidence, but no sooner had he been relieved of the captaincy than Botham started producing the old magic again, and almost single-handedly destroyed Kim Hughes's Australian team. Other friends pointed out the sad history of Pakistan captains over the years – a tale of woe, with most of them having been mistreated in some way. Either the Board had got at them, or the press had been merciless in its treatment of them.

It must be understood that there is a great divide in Pakistan

49

cricket between the two major centres, Karachi and Lahore. According to the parochial press, either Pakistan's Karachi-born captain was discriminating against Lahore-based players, or *vice versa*. However the team was selected, the two press factions would find something to argue about. The same thing happens in India, where the two main power bases are centred on Bombay and Delhi, and to a lesser extent in England as well, but on a North v South basis.

Finally, I was worried because Pakistan teams have always been difficult to handle. For some reason, Pakistani – and Indian – players seem to be more individualistic in their approach to the game than those from other countries. There are always a number of self-promoting candidates for captaincy within the team, and there is nothing more detrimental to team spirit than for the reigning captain to discover that there are several aspiring captains in his team. The moment the team loses, small pressure groups form within the side. In every team there will be the odd discontented person. I first noticed this on my first tour of England in 1971. During the third Test at Leeds, Pakistan had every chance of victory, and I became more and more tense as the climax approached. I was stunned to hear two of our players, who were not playing in the match, express the hope that certain of their colleagues would fail so that they would stand a better chance of Test selection. It didn't seem to matter to them whether Pakistan won or lost. This attitude often reared its head during subsequent tours by Pakistan. Obviously some teams were more cohesive than others, but I felt in general that the players lacked determination and a feeling of team unity. Once or twice I remember seeing players who harboured ambitions for the captaincy expressing pleasure at our losing because that would advance their hopes. I could never understand such an attitude.

Despite all my reservations, I eventually decided to accept. I did so because I realised that it was a great challenge, and also because I remembered that during my time at Oxford – my only other experience of team captaincy at first-class level – my own performances had improved with the responsibility of leading the side. I had led Oxford in 1974, and had started the season in good form, with a hundred in each innings against Nottinghamshire, 5 for 56 against Warwickshire, 5 for 96 against Derbyshire and 170 against Northants, whom we beat; and when captaining Oxford and Cambridge against the Indian tourists, I had hit 160 and 49, and taken 4 for 69. I realised that captaining Pakistan would be vastly different from leading Oxford, but after a good deal of thought I decided that I should take the job.

My decision was also helped by memories of our dreadful tour of Australia in 1981–2. There had been no team spirit on that trip, which was conducted almost throughout in a haze of bickering and argument. I knew I could do a better job than that, and could at least ensure that team selection was better organised. As for team spirit, it couldn't be any worse than it had been on that tour.

Zaheer, who was playing county cricket, called me up and did not hide his disappointment: he was very honest about it.

From the moment I accepted the captaincy I was determined that I would not be left out of the selection process, and I insisted on being consulted. I also knew that I would have to find a way of restoring the harmony in the dressing-room after the events of the preceding twelve months.

We started the tour in remarkable fashion, with confident performances in the first-class matches which preceded the first Test. Abdul Qadir, for whose selection I had fought really hard, bamboozled the county batsmen and received rave reviews in England. I was delighted because, just as I was leaving for England to join Sussex in April, I had bumped into Qadir at the Lahore Gymkhana nets. He seemed very disillusioned, and I was shocked when he talked in terms of giving up cricket and concentrating on business. He had failed in England in 1978, in India in 1979 and against the West Indies on spinning wickets in Pakistan. He had been dropped midway through the series and had not been considered since. I couldn't understand why he had failed, because whenever I played against him, whether in a match or in the nets, I had always found him difficult to read, whereas I never had much of a problem with Mushtaq and Intikhab. However, I knew that Intikhab had caused problems for a good many English batsmen, so Qadir might well be more effective if he could introduce more variety into his bowling. Mudassar and I encouraged him and told him that, whoever was the captain, we would press his case, and that he should start working hard. I also knew that the English batsmen played orthodox spin and medium pace better than most. Now it seemed I'd been proved right.

On the eve of the first Test I was extremely tense and I hardly slept. I felt sure that there were a great many people in Pakistan waiting to see me fail. I had had my first taste of the viciousness of the press when I was injured on the Indian tour of 1979 and Pakistan had lost, and Kapil was chosen the man of the series. And because I, along with the rest of the team, had refused to play under Javed Miandad, a section of the Karachi press had attacked my appointment as captain on a regional basis, because a Karachi captain had been dislodged by a Lahorite. I also suspected that a lot of people were expecting me to fail in the same way that Botham had flopped as a player when he was made captain. There was also the prospect of my first duel with Botham in a Test match.

But what worried me more than anything else was proving myself in front of my team. Except for one season at Oxford, I had never been a captain, yet I was now captaining a team which had revolted against its previous captain, and included three former captains and three former vice-captains among the regular Test eleven. Whenever a new captain is appointed, the team – like the public – gives him a chance, but only respects him if he is good enough to take it. No one can ever demand respect in sport through authority or threats. So for a while I kept a low profile in team meetings, leaving Intikhab, the manager, to do most of the talking.

There was another reason for my feeling anxious. Before this first Test as captain I had made an agonising personal decision. Majid Khan, who was my cousin and had helped me a lot in my early cricket, had not been scoring many runs in the county matches: after a good deal of thought I decided to leave him out of the Test side. It was like dropping my elder brother: what made it worse was that it was almost the first time he had been left out of the Test side since becoming a regular player. It was dreadful, but there was really no justification for including him in place of one of the younger batsmen who had been making runs.

We should have won that first Test at Edgbaston but let it slip out of our hands time and again. I had a good spell in England's first innings, taking 7 wickets for 52 runs, and England were dismissed for 272. I also won what was seen as a personal duel of all-rounders when I clean-bowled Ian Botham for 2. Our batting let us down, however: we had still not learned how to cope with the pressure of Test matches. Mudassar, who had made a lot of runs in the early matches, was l.b.w. in a really peculiar manner when he turned his back on a ball from Botham and was given out in one of the poorer decisions in Test cricket. Javed was playing well when he chose to try and hoist Hemmings out of the ground and was caught. We had frittered away the advantage we had gained in the field, and England took a lead of 21 runs into the second innings, in which their score of 291 was based on a lucky century by Randall. A superb spell from Tahir Naqqash destroyed the middle order, and at 212 for 9 we had them on the run, but Bob Willis and Bob Taylor added a vital 79 for the last wicket. They were beaten on innumerable occasions, but their luck held. Even so, we were in with a good chance to win the game, but our batting gave another depressingly familiar display. It lacked resolve, and our players seemed quite over-awed by the occasion. England reduced us to 97 for 7. With the match all but lost I played an innings of 65 that taught me a lot about how to bat in the lower order – in fact it turned out to be a watershed in my batting in Test matches. We lost by 113 runs; during this match I realised that I would have to put a lot more effort and concentration into my batting because our line-up was suspect, and I would have to lead by example.

Mohsin Khan made a superb double-century in the second Test at Lord's. Mansoor Akhtar and Zaheer also contributed useful fifties, bringing our score to over 400. Interrupted by intermittent rain, we managed to bowl out England for 227, two runs short of avoiding the follow-on. We had lost a good deal of time through bad weather, and the second Test would certainly have been drawn if England had not followed on. Qadir produced a magnificent spell and was largely responsible for making short work of the late-order batsmen. Even so, we had our work cut out dismissing England again, still more so since both Tahir and Sarfraz were injured and unable to bowl much. We were left with only two frontline bowlers, Qadir and myself. Both of us sent down approximately 60 overs in the match. It looked as though England would save the game, until Mudassar produced a devastating spell of medium-pace bowling, taking 6 for 32, as a result of which he was dubbed 'the man with the golden arm'. We were left to make 77 runs and got there in failing light, with 29 balls to spare. This was Pakistan's second victory in England – and the first ever at Lord's – and it had taken twenty-eight years to achieve it. The players and our fans were ecstatic. I was pleased by the doggedness of the whole team, which more than made up for the time we had lost due to rain.

In the third and final Test we won the toss and batted first on a bright sunny morning at Headingley. The wicket was playing relatively easily at this stage but, after a good start, our batsmen were unable to take full advantage of the first-day conditions. Although Mudassar, Javed and I made fifties, we managed only 275, and it was again up to our bowlers to get us back into the match. The Headingley wicket always helps seam bowling, and we were unlucky that injuries to Sarfraz and Tahir kept them out of the game. Had we had Sarfraz's experience to help us, I think we would have won the match. We had to summon Ehteshamuddin, who was playing league cricket in England, to fill the gap. He gave his best but was not fit enough. It was largely up to me to provide the firepower to bowl out England. I took five wickets, and Sikander chipped in with a couple, and we managed to secure a lead of 19 runs.

In our second innings Javed made another fine fifty, but the rest of our top order didn't do anything. Both the openers, Mohsin and Mudassar, got ducks. At 128 for 7 the match seemed more or less over, until I shared a partnership of 41 with Qadir. Sikander Bakht was giving me useful assistance for the ninth wicket when he was unfortunate enough to be given out by the umpire, David Constant – a truly bizarre decision, because his bat was nowhere near the ball. As a result, England were left with 219 to win. They started in confident fashion and their openers, Chris Tavaré and Graeme Fowler, put on 103 for the first wicket. England needed only 47 runs, with eight wickets in hand, when Mudassar began his second magic spell of the series. I took a couple of wickets as well, and England declined from 172 for 2 to 189 for 6 before bad light ended play. By now their confidence had gone, and we might have bowled them out that evening but for the weather. Next morning they needed about 25 runs, with four wickets in hand, but were in a calmer frame of mind and won the match by three wickets.

Although we had performed well above expectations, I was understandably disappointed, because I knew that with a little more grit we could easily have won this series. The amount of bowling I had done had taken a lot out of me physically, and I felt completely drained by the end of the tour. The good news was that the pressures of captaincy had actually raised the level of my performance, and I was made the man of the series. That winter we were due to play two series, comprising nine Test matches, against Australia and India.

The series against Australia really belonged to one man – Abdul Qadir. None of the Australian batsmen could read him, and he took 22 wickets in the three Tests. In England the media had been enthralled by Qadir's bowling, and declared him a great spinner. I couldn't believe it when I returned to Pakistan and found that certain sections of the Karachi press were attacking Qadir for his bowling on the English tour. In fact he had bowled very well and had been unlucky not to get more wickets. English umpires – like English batsmen – often failed to read his googly and flipper, and were reluctant to give the batsman out l.b.w. A section of the Karachi press chose to ignore this and claimed that he was only in the side because he had my support.

During the first Test against Australia in Karachi, Qadir was actually booed and pelted when he entered the ground. This was the man about whom John Arlott, the great English commentator and cricket writer, had said that just to watch Qadir bowl had made his summer. Now, destroying Australia, Qadir silenced his detractors. Back on familiar pitches, the Pakistani batsmen made a good many runs, and we comprehensively beat Australia 3-0. We won two Tests by nine wickets and the other by an innings. I found it extremely difficult to inspire myself throughout this series. The Australians usually come to the sub-continent during the off-season when it is still hot and the pitches are completely brown. Both the weather and the pitches take a lot out of fast bowlers. This practice of playing in September and October should be discouraged: the Australians can get away with it because they are prepared to pay so much money to get teams to visit them in their own season.

CHAPTER 5

Pain

On the second day of the second Test against India at Karachi in December 1982, I got out of bed and felt a pain in my left shin bone. We had bowled the previous day and I had not experienced any discomfort, and I could not recall any incident on the field that might have caused it. I decided that I must have knocked my leg somehow, and when I got to the ground and started warming up, the pain gradually disappeared and I forgot about it. Little did I know that it would transform my career, my life and the shape of Pakistan cricket for the next two years.

The following day, as I warmed up, the pain reappeared, and I began to suspect that it might not be an ordinary bruise. We had dismissed India cheaply on the first day, and then accumulated a large total thanks to centuries by Mudassar and Zaheer. I felt no discomfort while batting, and I was at the crease for some time. With India batting again, almost 300 behind, the pain reappeared when I bowled – but I had been playing non-stop cricket for many months, and had had a number of niggling injuries. I still hoped that this was just another of them.

I began a new spell after tea, with India well set at 100 for 1, and Gavaskar and Vengsarkar going well. After a couple of overs the pain disappeared and, in any case, I probably would not have noticed it in the general euphoria of the next hour and a half. It was cooler, there was a cross breeze, and the ball was swinging, as it tends to in the evenings at Karachi. Once I had bowled Gavaskar, the Indian innings folded, with most of my wickets coming from fast inswingers, or 'indippers' as some commentators called them. India collapsed to 114 for 7, and I took 5 for 7. We wrapped up the match early on the fourth day, winning by an innings, and I had taken 8 for 60, Pakistan's best analysis against India and the record for a Karachi Test.

Naturally I was elated, both as a player and as a captain. I had not mentioned the pain to anyone except Mudassar, who agreed with my theory that I must have bumped my leg. So I proceeded unconcerned to the third Test, at Faisalabad. I was then at my peak as a fast bowler: all the hard work I had put in was paying off. I felt I had never been so fit in my life, and knew that I could sustain long spells of consistently hostile bowling. Faisalabad is normally considered a fast bowler's graveyard, but I produced one of the best performances of my career. On a placid Iqbal Stadium pitch, I had a match analysis of 11 for 180 in 55.5 overs, against an Indian batting line-up rated by some as the best in the world.

India batted first and scored 372, normally a good first-innings total. Then, for the first time, four Pakistanis scored centuries in the same Test innings as we recorded 652, our highest total against India; Zaheer, who had scored 215 and 186 in the first two Tests, made 168, and I hit 117, including ten fours and five sixes. I hit 21 in one over off Kapil Dev, who conceded over 200 runs in the innings. When India batted again, Sarfraz and I made early inroads, and they were soon 48 for 3. After that it was just a matter of time, and we won by 10 wickets. In the match I equalled Ian Botham's record – also set against India – of scoring a century and taking 10 wickets in the same Test.

By now I could feel the pain even when batting. The ball was keeping low and, because I was constantly on the front foot, I was often hit on the shin: for a time I blamed the problem on sub-standard pads. Eventually I consulted a physiotherapist, who said it was just a bruise. I did not want anything to interrupt our progress in the series, so I accepted his diagnosis and went to Hyderabad for the next Test, where, on the easiest of batting pitches, we ran up 581 for 3 declared. Mudassar and Javed both hit double centuries, and put on 451 for the third wicket, equalling the Test record for any wicket. Once again the Indian batting crumpled, declining from 44 for 1 to 72 for 7. I bowled what I still consider to be my fastest-ever spell, taking 5 for 3 in the space of a few overs.

After this the pain got worse. A lump appeared on my shin bone, and I kept having to spray the area to dull the pain before bowling. Even so, the agony was intense: I kept bowling until I had crossed the pain barrier, but as soon as I stopped I could hardly stand. After my efforts in the first innings, when I took six wickets, I was unable to bowl properly in a Test match for three years. My run-up became tentative and I was unable to put much weight on the front foot.

We won by an innings at Hyderabad, and so led 3-0 in the series, with two matches to play. With the series won, I could have opted out of the last two Tests, but the cause of the problem had not yet been diagnosed. Some x-rays were taken in Lahore, after the last two days of the fifth Test had been washed out, but unfortunately no one in Pakistan had any experience of 'stress' fractures of the shin bone. Repeated loads applied to parts of the skeleton sometimes produce lesions known as 'stress' or 'fatigue' fractures – an injury often found among marathon runners. The bone in question becomes painful and tender. Radiologically, the fracture is invisible at first, which was why the doctors I consulted initially thought it a bad case of bruising.

The final two Tests were boring draws, and despite the now intense pain in my leg I bowled 66 overs. Only my experience and the Indian batsmen's lack of confidence prevented me from getting a hiding. At times I was visibly limping in my run-up. Despite my problems, I took seven wickets in the last two Tests, to finish with 40 in the series at an average of 13.95, easily my best series aggregate. I also scored 247 runs, averaging 61.75.

After the series I again showed my leg to a doctor, who trotted out the familiar diagnosis of bad bruising. This was a crucial error: had I received accurate advice at this point and rested the leg, it would have healed comparatively quickly. Although I hardly bowled at all during the next few months, I kept running, which merely aggravated the injury.

When I eventually discovered that I would not be able to bowl for a while, my immediate reaction was one of relief. The pain I had suffered had been so intense that the mere thought of bowling repelled me. On 1 April 1983, new x-rays revealed a huge crack in my shin bone. The specialist said it was one of the worst cases of stress fracture he had seen: he was amazed that the bone had not shattered completely under the pressure I had placed on it, and it would take up to a year to heal. I very much wanted to play in the 1983 World Cup in England, and the doctor said that there was a possibility that I could play solely as a batsman.

I was prepared to forgo the World Cup if that meant that I would be fully fit for Pakistan's tour of Australia that winter, but the BCCP asked me to play in the World Cup as a batsman if at all possible. I was worried, because I had never played for Pakistan as a specialist batsman before; nor had I turned out in county cricket for Sussex that summer, and so had not had any match practice.

Our batting for the World Cup was no longer the star-studded line-up of previous years, and the bowling attack too was ordinary. I insisted that Qadir was selected, even though it was not fashionable to include a leg-spinner in one-day international sides, and he proved to be the success of the World Cup for us. We qualified for the semi-finals, partly due to brilliant bowling by Qadir in two of the matches, and also thanks to Sri Lanka's surprise win over New Zealand in their last match.

I managed to finish top of our batting averages, which partly resolved my own doubts, but the satisfaction of batting well could not compensate for the frustration of watching helplessly while our bowlers were getting thrashed. In the semi-finals we were defeated by the West Indies, who went on to lose the final to India – a fact that did not go down well with the

Pakistan press, which expressed its anger by attacking my captaincy and team selection. For my part, I thought it a miracle that we reached the semi-final with the team we had.

After the World Cup I played for Sussex. My batting continued to improve, and I finished the season with an average of about 60, my best ever. The specialist told me I could start bowling a few overs off a short run-up. I really enjoyed the four-over spells I was allowed, and took the first hat-trick of my career against Warwickshire.

Looking back, I think that if my specialist had really understood the mechanics of bowling, he would not have let me attempt it. After the Warwickshire match the pain returned, although x-rays seemed to indicate that the healing process was continuing, but further x-rays – following a short tour of Jamaica – showed unmistakably that the fracture had opened up again.

My frustration was intense. Clearly the bone was not going to mend easily, and there was little chance of my being able to bowl properly on the Australian tour. I had really been looking forward to bowling on the quick Aussie pitches, but even worse was the fact that without me our attack would struggle, lacking that edge of pace so vital on Australian wickets.

In my absence Pakistan, led by Zaheer Abbas, had played an uninspiring three-Test series against India, all the matches being drawn. I informed the BCCP that I was available to go to Australia as a batsman; they felt that my performance the previous winter had shown the right qualities: I was to captain the team in Australia. I was a little hesitant, and had my doubts about the wisdom of the move, but the prospect of returning to Australia, as well as my recent success as a batsman, overrode my doubts. I also felt that I could captain the side much better than Zaheer, whose approach to the game, like Boycott's, was too cautious and self-absorbed.

No sooner had I accepted the captaincy than a selection dispute erupted. The inexperienced opener Shoaib Moham-mad, Hanif's son, had been included. There was no good reason for his inclusion at that stage of his career, especially as there were others far more deserving of a place. However, Shoaib had the backing of a number of selectors, and the dispute led to the resignation of the selection committee and a split in the BCCP. A pressure group was formed which, together with certain sections of the Karachi press, made my appointment as captain a point of issue. Feeling that Zaheer would be more responsive to their interests, they argued that I should go as a batsman under his captaincy. Nothing came of this, but the unsavoury controversy was to colour the whole tour, and have a pernicious influence on post-tour events as well.

In retrospect, it is obvious that I should not have gone to Australia without being fully fit. Pakistan's cricket bureaucracy had long been used to controlling every aspect of the game, and they resented the diminution of certain aspects of their power during my tenure as captain. For them, my failure in Australia was a heaven-sent opportunity.

Soon after my arrival in Australia I consulted a specialist in Brisbane, and the x-rays he took led him to recommend that I should not even bat for two months. I sought a second opinion, which supported his diagnosis. I discussed the matter with Intikhab Alam, the tour manager, who had become a close friend, and we immediately relayed the doctors' opinions to the BCCP. They told me to stay with the team and take my place in due course. Zaheer, the vice-captain, took over the responsibilities of captaincy, and his first act was to issue a statement that this was not the team he would have chosen, and that he was only a caretaker captain. Intikhab and I asked him what sort of team he wanted, but on this score he was ambiguous and evasive: he just kept repeating that this was not his team. This was a peculiar attitude, because he knew that a vice-captain's duties might include taking over in the captain's absence. It was probably a ploy to avoid all responsibility if we lost.

We did lose the first Test, at Perth, by an innings. On a fast, bouncy pitch we let Australia score over 400, and were then bundled out for 129 and 298 by Lillee, Hogg, Rackemann and

Lawson. In the second Test we batted first and were again dismissed cheaply. In reply, Australia made 509 for 7, and only a thunderstorm, which washed out the last day and a half, saved us from another defeat. By now the BCCP was under pressure to appoint Zaheer as tour captain: they wilted under the pressure, but to everyone's surprise he rejected the offer, repeating that he was merely a caretaker and that he would relinquish the captaincy as soon as I was fit.

In the third Test our batting finally clicked, and we responded to Australia's 465 with 624. When they batted again, Australia were in some difficulty at 121 for 3, but we could not press home the advantage and they batted out time for a draw. After this match my leg was again x-rayed, and although there was no significant improvement the doctor felt that I could start batting again. I batted in the nets for hours and then played against Tasmania, where I promptly failed in both innings. This put me in a quandary, because I could hardly drop a batsman after the huge score in the previous Test. But it was essential for me to justify my presence on the tour, so I omitted the off-spinner Nazir Junior. He had taken 1 for 217 in the first three Tests, so I thought his absence wouldn't make much difference.

I have never felt so nervous going into a Test match. If I failed as a batsman, or if one of our bowlers was injured while we were on top, I would be letting the team and my country down. I usually approach each match in a positive and constructive frame of mind, but this time I was not optimistic. On the eve of the match Dennis Lillee, with whom I have always enjoyed a good relationship, somehow read my mind. He told me that very few people take risks, and that those who do gain a lot – although it can always go the other way.

We batted first and got off to a good start, thanks to a brilliant century from Mohsin Khan. I went in thirty minutes before stumps, just before Australia took the second new ball, and had made 10 by the close. I could hardly sleep that night, but the following day I relaxed and gradually began to play with confidence. By the time Lillee produced one of his unplayable outswingers I had made 83. We totalled 470, but Australia topped this with 555, largely thanks to Graham Yallop, a master of the type of bowling we possessed, who made 268. In our second innings we collapsed to 81 for 5, at which point I played the best innings of my career. I managed 72 not out, holding our innings together, and we saved the match.

A huge load was lifted from my shoulders by this performance. In the glow of success, I chose to ignore the pain in my leg, which had increased throughout the match – I had batted for a long time, and fielded through Australia's big innings.

Pakistan lost the last Test, in Sydney, by 10 wickets, the match following the by now familiar pattern. Australia scored 454 for 6, and dismissed us twice for 278 and 210. This was their last Test for three tremendous cricketers – Greg Chappell, Dennis Lillee and Rod Marsh. It was a moment of great sadness. In 1972, when I was just a schoolboy, these three had formed the nucleus of the great Australian team which dominated world cricket for years.

New x-rays revealed that the wound had opened up again. The doctor advised me to go home and rest for four months. Zaheer had already gone back, saying that he needed to work on his benefit, but on his return he wrote a column criticising the team selection and my leadership: he was preparing the ground for assuming the captaincy himself in the near future. In these circumstances I felt that if I also left the team it would collapse completely, so I stayed on for the World Series Cup one-day competition. This series proved to be a nightmare. We lost all but one of our ten matches, I couldn't bowl, and we were completely outplayed. I got a few runs at first but missed the later matches, when Javed Miandad captained the team.

The whole experience was torture. I had given my critics all the ammunition they needed to attack me and the Board. Looking back, it is easy to say that I should not have gone, but in some ways the tour was a character-building experience. I also learned a lot about my team mates – which ones I could rely on, and which were fair-weather friends.

I returned from Australia to rest at home. There was an

almost constant barrage of criticism pouring out from our press. As expected, the Board was toppled and the opposition group took over. Zaheer was appointed captain and I was condemned by the press. I found this hard to take and became bitter: all that I had done, as captain and player, seemed to have been forgotten. The new Board treated me with disdain, like a spoilt child who needed to be put in his place. They had always resented the fact that I had not been prepared to grovel before them, and now that it seemed I was finished all the knives came out.

Zaheer continued writing his column in *Dawn*, in which he sniped at my captaincy and lobbied to be chosen as my successor. Meanwhile, one of the players accused me of being unfair in team selection and of having dropped him for no reason. The new BCCP administration told the press that the senior players had made money on the tour and that I had used my authority to deprive the junior ones of their rightful financial benefits. The slander and innuendo were seemingly endless, and there was no way in which I could respond on the field.

In March 1984, another round of x-rays suggested that my career was indeed over. I was to get out of cricket, like so many other great Pakistani players of the past, abandoned and abused. The prospect of never playing again was depressing, but even harder to face was the fact that I had been humiliated and would never get the chance to redeem myself.

My cousin, Dr Farrukh, spoke to the Punjab health minister, Hamid Nasir Chatta, who immediately convened a meeting of the top orthopaedic surgeons of Lahore. One of the participants suggested a form of treatment which was still at an experimental stage, whereby the healing process was hastened by means of electrical cycles passed through the leg. As the bone was no longer healing, I decided that I was willing to try anything that would give me an opportunity to play again. The treatment recommended was expensive, but was fortunately subsidised by the government on General Zia's personal recommendation.

I went to England in April, and met Dr Beard at the Cromwell Hospital in London. He told me that the minimum time required for the treatment would be six months, that my leg would have to be put in a cast, and that I was to take no exercise at all. For ten hours a day I could hardly move. The instrument inserted in the cast had to be plugged in to produce the therapeutic electrical cycles. This was probably the most difficult period of my life. It is not easy for a sportsman accustomed to perpetual exercise to adapt to being completely deprived of it.

At the same time I was extremely depressed and bitter about the way I had been treated by the cricketing community in Pakistan. For six weeks I hardly left my flat in London. I was so put off by the criticism I had received that I stopped following cricket in the newspapers or watching it on television. I did nothing but read and wallow in self-pity. In these difficult weeks, Emma Sergeant, a well-known painter and a good friend of mine, gave me great support. Slowly I began to emerge from my self-imposed hermitage. A friend quoted an old Chinese proverb: 'A bitter man is a man who is lost in life.' I started thinking more calmly and rationally about the events of the previous year. I realised that I had taken a big risk in going to Australia, and that it hadn't paid off. I should have known that I would be crucified if I failed. Even my anger with Zaheer began to fade: after all, he had never hidden his fierce desire to become captain of Pakistan. I mellowed as a person and became more tolerant. In the past I could not easily have forgiven anyone, a very typical Pathan characteristic. Now I learned how to look through other people's eyes and understand them better.

I started going out again and made new friends, and began to realise that there was a life outside cricket. The people I was meeting had nothing to do with the game. For the first time since Oxford I met people outside cricket with whom I had much in common. Initially I found it difficult and mostly listened, but their company was stimulating and I was soon an enthusiastic participant in their conversations and activities.

My old core of friends stood by me. I've had few but fast friendships, and I am still extremely close to some of the people I met in this period. My natural optimism began to assert itself: instinct told me that I would play again, although most people thought otherwise. Three months after my leg was put in a cast, a new set of x-rays showed only marginal improvement, yet I continued to hope that all would be well. I even began to watch cricket on television again. This period of my life left me with much that was to prove useful later on, and it also helped to prepare me for my retirement. For one thing, I came to realise how fickle public adulation can be. Despite all the difficulties of that time, I'm sure I would have been worse off without it. I emerged from it much stronger as a person, and with a far wider perspective on life.

CHAPTER 6

Comeback

1 October 1984 was a red-letter day in my life. The x-rays showed that my leg had healed completely. The doctor did not guarantee that there would be no reversal, and for a long time doubts still lingered in my mind. I was allowed to start training again. I'll never forget my first run in Hyde Park – I felt like a bird freed from its cage. In fact, I still run the same stretch in the park whenever I go there. I had already prepared the ground for my return to first-class cricket. In July, while watching Wimbledon, I had met Linton Taylor from PBL Marketing, whom I knew from the Packer days. We had talked about my return, and I had signed a contract to play for New South Wales that winter, provided I was fit. There were two reasons for my wanting to restart my cricket career in Australia. I was keen that my progress should be monitored by a leading Australian specialist; and I did not want to play in or for Pakistan until I was fully fit again.

The pleasure I felt at my recovery was dulled by my mother's illness. She had developed cancer and was in England undergoing treatment. I spent most of my time with her and the rest playing at the indoor nets at Lord's. In October I left for Australia, where I was warmly received by the New South Wales Cricket Association, and in particular its secretary, Bob Radford. I began by playing Grade cricket for Sydney University. During my first match for them against Waverley, I felt the old pain in my leg return, so I immediately contacted the specialist who was following my progress. He told me that I should expect some discomfort to begin with and that I should carry on playing. I did just that and, although the pain continued, I did not confide in anyone. By this time I had decided that there was no point in agonising over it. If the wound opened up again there was very little I could do about it and my career would be over. I decided to continue playing come what may.

I wasn't immediately picked to play for New South Wales. Not until the arrival of the West Indian touring team did I start to play for them, and in that match – which we won – I took three wickets, and made a few runs. I then played for NSW against Queensland in December, bowling 40 overs in the match. At this time I was bowling medium-pace line and length. I was given a lot of encouragement by the NSW players, even though I wasn't yet able to perform up to my previous standards. I used to bowl long spells just to see how much my leg could take: sometimes the pain was quite severe, but the heartening thing was that it didn't get any worse beyond a certain point. After a while it began to lessen, and I knew that I was on my way back.

I spent the next month shuttling between Australia and Pakistan. My mother's condition had deteriorated, and I spent two weeks at home, went back to Australia and then returned home in January, where I remained until she died. I had always been very close to my mother, and had I not been playing cricket this would have been a much more difficult time for me.

By now I was a regular member of the NSW team. Somehow I just couldn't bowl as fast as I used to, and this puzzled me. In the match against Tasmania, I experimented with my bowling action but couldn't figure out what was wrong: I stayed up all night to work it out in my mind. I analysed my action stage by stage, and eventually, by a process of elimination, I decided that there were three things I might possibly be doing wrong. The next morning I arrived very early at the nets and bowled for almost an hour before the start of the match. I thought perhaps I was not leaning back enough before delivering the ball, or not jumping high enough at the point of delivery, but neither idea worked. In the end, I discovered that I had lost something far more subtle, as a result of bowling off a short run-up. Previously I had made a kind of double-circular – or, more accurately, one-and-a-half revolutions – movement of my bowling arm as I went into the final jump. The short run had cut this movement and simultaneously reduced the jump because the body was not cocked up sufficiently. I bowled for long spells in the match, and by the fourth day I had got it right.

It was an extremely successful season for NSW. I played for them in the McDonald's Cup and the Sheffield Shield final, and we won both. In the same length of time as a county season there were less than half the number of four-day first-class matches and a quarter as many one-day games. A Shield match was approached with enormous enthusiasm, even by those cricketers who were part of the national team. I was struck by the competitiveness and the aggression with which such matches were played – a far cry from the tranquillity of the three-day county match in England. One particular Shield match, between New South Wales and Queensland, was more competitive than many Test matches I had played. Both sides included Australian Test candidates, who had been playing together the previous week against the West Indies. Now they were at each other's throats, and a lot of verbal abuse was being exchanged.

One of the best games of cricket I have ever watched was between Western Australia and Queensland in a one-day match. The Western Australians were bowled out for 70, and Dennis Lillee bowled out Queensland for even less. The Queensland side included Greg Chappell and Viv Richards. I remember Dennis Lillee telling me that on occasions he enjoyed playing for Western Australia more than in Test matches.

It's not surprising that Australia manages to produce such outstanding teams despite playing so few first-class matches. It's the quality that counts. Their first-class cricket is the nearest thing to Test cricket. The emphasis is not on line and length but on getting wickets. The middle-order batsmen get a chance to play big innings; flat spinners and medium-pacers are ineffective.

But I found that Australian cricketers tended to be tactically unsound. Grade cricket, which feeds the Shield teams, is competitive, but too infrequent. It is played over weekends – and usually only on a Saturday. Since the matches depend on first-innings leads, one team bowls on one Saturday, and the other has to wait its turn the following Saturday. For a young batsman, one innings over two weeks is too infrequent. Moreover, most Grade grounds have football played on them during the winter, and they don't recover from the ravages of the football season until the middle of the cricket season. Not surprisingly, a lot of the cricket is of poor standard.

It was also the year of the World Championship of Cricket in Australia, and at last I felt confident enough to play for Pakistan again. We had completed a losing series in New Zealand, and the team was to play in the competition on its way back. We reached the final of the tournament and then lost to India, who had also beaten us in a group match. After this I played for Pakistan in the Four-Nations tournament in Sharjah. In the match against India I bowled what was probably my best one-day spell, taking 6 for 14 in 10 overs. India were dismissed for only 125, but what should have been a walk-over was transformed into defeat by incredibly spineless batting, and we were bowled out for only 87. My experience with the team in the one-day tournaments in Australia and Sharjah showed me that there was no commitment or team spirit left. Everyone was playing for himself because no one had any confidence in the selection process, and players were only interested in retaining their own places.

I went back to England to play for Sussex that summer, returning to Pakistan after the county season. That October the Sri Lankan team toured Pakistan and we beat them easily enough 2-0. I got nine wickets in the second Test and made a fair number of runs. Despite my performance, I found the series rather dull because of its one-sided nature. The Sri Lankans, who had recently beaten India at home, made an issue of the biased umpiring and the bad facilities. I can well imagine that the facilities were inadequate because Rafi Naseem, the BCCP secretary, was a terrible administrator. The umpiring was not that bad; we were simply a better team. The Sri Lankans, who had beaten India at home, had come to Pakistan with a completely misguided estimate of their abilities.

During the Sri Lankan tour, Javed Miandad announced that he would step down from the captaincy once the tour was over. He had been criticised remorselessly for the team's showing in Australia, New Zealand and Sharjah. We had lost three consecutive one-day internationals to India, which the public in Pakistan always found hard to accept. He didn't have the stomach to lead Pakistan against India again in Sharjah, or against the West Indies in the forthcoming one-day series in Pakistan. I was reappointed captain, and I knew that I would have to remould the side completely after the ravages of the previous year. In Sharjah we beat India for the first time that year, but lost the tournament to the West Indies. We came back home and played a thrilling cliffhanger of a one-day series with the West Indies which we lost 3-2 – a commendable performance against easily the best team in the world.

The tour of Sri Lanka early in 1986 was even more unpleasant than the 1979 tour of Australia. Before the tour began, the BCCP tried to pressure me by delaying the announcement of the captain and the team until four days before the team left on tour. I issued a statement that I would not go if I was not given the team I wanted, which they accepted. In the one-day series against the West Indies I had tried to establish the nucleus of a team for the next two years. The series provided an ideal opportunity for building up team spirit, and finding gutsy, determined players. I did not want all this good work undone by the labyrinthine workings of Pakistan's selection process.

As soon as we arrived in Sri Lanka we were taken aback by the hostility of the media and the public. We learnt that Duleep Mendis, the Sri Lankan captain, had given such a biased

account of his team's tour of Pakistan that the entire country
was up in arms against us before a ball had been bowled.
Pakistan's ambassador to Sri Lanka told us that he had
telegraphed the BCCP and advised them not to send the team,
because he felt that the atmosphere was not conducive to a
tour.

Not until we played the first Test did we understand what
was in store for us. On the first morning of the match, before it
was barely half an hour old, umpire Felsinger, while turning
down an appeal, told us to shut up and get on with the game.
He added that this was 'not Pakistan'. Arjuna Ranatunga was
given at least half a dozen lives by the umpires. In frustration,
our close-in fielders called him a cheat and he walked off the
ground, taking the umpires with him. I was later told by the
Indians that the same thing had happened to them when they
were beaten by Sri Lanka. He wanted an apology from me. I
asked him why he had provoked the players by telling them
that 'This is not Pakistan'. He said he hadn't. So I told him that
if he hadn't then neither had anyone called him a cheat. The
match was resumed and we beat them by an innings in spite of
countless umpiring decisions against us. Wettimuny walked,
even though the umpire had not given him out, and we learned
that he was criticised by his team for doing so. When I heard
this I lost all respect for the Sri Lankan captain and players. We
also discovered that the biased umpiring was part of a plan.
Even though our first four batsmen were given out l.b.w., we
won the match by an innings. The pitch at Kandy was a turner,
and Sri Lanka did not possess any good spinners. We had
Qadir and Tauseef, who bowled them out for 109 and 101 –
Tauseef taking nine wickets.

The first match had been at Kandy, in the hills, so when we
played the second Test at Colombo, we were completely
unprepared for the fierce, clammy heat. The tour itinerary was
such that we had no time at all in which to acclimatise. After
three or four overs our bowlers looked wiped out. We did not
play well in the second Test and the umpiring was a travesty.
When Javed was given out he almost had a punch-up with the

Sri Lankan players, and as he was returning to the pavilion someone threw a stone at him; he ran into the crowd to punish the offender and the other players followed to protect him. At the end of the day's play we all agreed that there was no point in continuing the tour. We drafted a statement to this effect, but General Zia called me up and told me to persuade the boys to complete the tour. By now our players knew that, given the umpiring, it would be difficult to get any runs or take wickets. However, we didn't play very well in the second Test, and the combination of our poor performance and the umpiring resulted in an easy win for Sri Lanka. In the third Test the umpiring was a little better, and we would have won the match if we had not dropped so many catches.

I had toured Sri Lanka in 1976 and found it a pleasant, friendly place in which to play cricket. In 1986 I thought I had come to a different country. The hostility was unrelenting and unanimous. Even the waiters in the hotel and the people in the streets were rude to us. It was as though the entire population was united in its determination to beat us at all costs, and be thoroughly unpleasant as well. Not a single voice was raised against the umpiring or the behaviour of the spectators. In Pakistan and elsewhere there are usually a few journalists or fellow-cricketers who point out these things when they become excessive. In Sri Lanka we felt as though we were locked in a darkened room without a chink of light. The Sri Lankans were obviously anxious to prove that they had come of age as a Test-playing country, but this in itself cannot explain the degree of antagonism we encountered. I think the civil war in Sri Lanka was responsible for a heightened patriotic fervour which, on the cricket field, was transmuted into a blind hatred of the opposition. The souring of a series due to an uncertain political situation or traditional enmity between two peoples was not new to me, but on this tour it was as bad as it could possibly have been.

The West Indies tour of Pakistan began the most important and exhilarating year of cricket of my whole career. When I came home at the end of the county season I knew that I was about to embark on a cricketing journey that would make or break my reputation as a player and as captain. After the West Indies tour we would go to India and then, in the summer, to England. The tour of England was to be followed immediately by the 1987 World Cup in the sub-continent, almost the last international fixture of my career. Three difficult Test series and a World Cup in twelve months: what a way to go! It was a tailor-made opportunity to fulfil my wildest cricketing dreams.

The first series, against the West Indies at home, looked the most difficult. Although Holding and Garner were missing, the pace attack of Marshall, Walsh, Patterson and Gray was formidable enough for Pakistan's still suspect batting order. Unlike ours, their batting line-up was strong and experienced, including Greenidge, Haynes, Richardson, Richards, Gomes and Dujon. The West Indies had beaten us easily on their previous tour. I knew that our batsmen, most of whom were relative newcomers, would find the sustained pace of the West Indians hard to handle. We hadn't done too badly in the one-day series a year earlier, but facing the same bowlers in a Test match was a different proposition. The underprepared pitches would certainly help our spinners, but because of the varied bounce the faster bowlers would also be dangerous.

We won the toss in the first Test at Faisalabad, and had the best of the pitch. I had told the batsmen that I didn't mind if they failed, but they would have to fight all the way, and I would not tolerate any lack of courage. On the first day of the series, the West Indian fast bowlers overawed our top order, and I came in to bat with the scoreboard reading 37 for 5. The very first ball I received from Marshall was a quick, sharply rearing delivery which hit me on the shoulder. Very soon my shoulder swelled up and became stiff. I realised that, if I went off, the team would be bowled out immediately and the match virtually over. Salim Malik and I were steadying the innings somewhat when a ball from Walsh broke Salim's arm. Qadir lasted for a while, as did Tauseef. I was the last to go, after making 61 from a total of 159.

When the West Indies came in to bat we fought them all the way and never let their batsmen get out of hand. Wasim Akram bowled accurately, taking 6 for 91, and we held them to a total of 248. In the second innings we lost two quick wickets on the second evening, and everyone thought the match would be over the next day. Then the whole batting order fought all the way down the line, and we reached 258 for 8 before Wasim Akram launched an assault on the West Indies fast bowlers. Earlier Salim Yousuf had played a gritty innings of 61, and now Salim Malik came out and batted for a long time with a cast on his broken arm. The West Indies began to look pretty ragged in the field. They knew that it would be difficult to get anything more than 200 in the fourth innings on a crumbling pitch. By the time they got us out we had a lead of 239.

The post-tea period on the fourth day was one of the most remarkable sessions of Test cricket I have ever played. A rising ball from Marshall had injured the index finger of my right hand, and it had taken three stitches to repair the damage. The finger was swollen and stiff and I could barely hold the ball, but I knew that we needed an early breakthrough, so I put everything into my opening spell. I was rewarded with the wickets of Haynes and Greenidge. The West Indies were now on the defensive: it was exactly the right moment in which to turn Qadir loose. Surrounded by close-in fieldsmen, the West Indies fell apart in the face of Qadir's leg-spin, and by the end of the day they were 43 for 9. The fifth day was a formality and they were bundled out for 53, their lowest-ever score in Tests. Qadir had taken 6 for 16 in 9.3 overs, and we had won the match by 186 runs.

The West Indies exacted quick revenge for their humiliation in the first Test, winning the second by an innings in three days. Marshall, Gray and Walsh dismissed us for 131 and 77 on a pitch which was not really quick. They made only 218 in their first innings, but this was enough to beat us without needing to bat again. Neither side had topped 300 more than once in seven completed innings so far. By the end of the second Test our batting was in tatters. We had not found any openers we could rely on, while of our middle-order batsmen, Qasim Omar and Salim Malik were injured and Qadir's hand had been broken while fielding.

Despite the fractured bone in his left hand, Qadir played in the third Test, and was instrumental in restricting the West Indies to a total of 240 in their first innings. Richards, who made a dogged and uncharacteristic 70, was the only one to play him with any confidence. In our turn, Rameez and Javed made patient fifties, and we totalled 239. After two and a half days the match was evenly balanced. On the third evening we missed a chance of winning the match, and the series, when Greenidge and Haynes were dropped very early in the West Indian innings. On the fourth day I produced my best bowling of the series as the West Indies slumped from 171 for 5 to 211 all out – I took 5 for 11 in 33 balls. But by the end of the fourth day our target of 230 looked a long way off after we had lost two wickets for 16 runs. Dogged, protracted defence by Rameez and Mudassar on the final day held up the West Indian advance. However, we were 125 for 7 when the umpires called off play because of bad light with nine of the mandatory twenty overs left to be bowled. At this point Tauseef and I were in the middle, desperately defending against some ferocious fast bowling. We had drawn the series by the skin of our teeth.

I was particularly proud of the team's performance because we had not only held the strongest team in the world, but had done so under the supervision of neutral Indian umpires. I had insisted on using neutral umpires in this series because touring teams had so often come to Pakistan and complained bitterly about the umpiring – and what had happened in Sri Lanka earlier in the year had strengthened my resolve. I didn't want our performance to be undermined by umpiring disputes. I think this was one of the few series ever played in Pakistan in which umpiring never became an issue. After this, on my prompting, we suggested to the ICC that neutral umpires should be used for all Test series, but most of the other Test-playing countries were uninterested. As a result, I have little sympathy for teams who complain about the umpiring.

It had been an exciting and satisfying series. In spite of ending in a draw, the third Test match at Karachi had been a tense, pressurised match, and the crowd had cheered our fight-back on the last day as if we were winning. In Salim Yousuf, Pakistan had found a courageous player, and one who could handle a crisis. Although our batting order was still somewhat fragile, the players had withstood the pressure. I felt confident that the team was now better prepared to face the rigours of a tour of India. My enemies in the BCCP had been silenced after our victory at Faisalabad. However, old habits die hard. I was in Australia with the team, taking part in the Perth Challenge – a one-day tournament staged as a sideshow to the America's Cup – when I heard that the squad for India had been announced in my absence. As captain I was part of the selection committee, and I was furious that I had not been consulted, still more so since I also felt that the team chosen lacked some of the qualities we would need in India. I had only taken on the captaincy after being assured that if I needed any changes once on tour, I would get them.

When we arrived in India I found that there was not as much publicity or interest in the tour as had been the case in 1979. There were a number of reasons for this. To begin with, this was the third series in India that season, and we had been squeezed in at the end, after the Australian and Sri Lankan teams. Secondly, our team, unlike that of 1979, was not rated very highly. Our batting was thought to be weak and inexperienced, and our bowling not strong enough to make much of an impact on the Indian batting in these conditions. Finally, the low-key, unfriendly reception we received reflected the border tension between the two countries at the time. All in all it was going to be a tough and tiring tour. In two months we would have to play five Tests, six one-day internationals, and some side games. And since it was an off-season tour we would also have to play in hot weather – particularly in the south, where we were due to play the first Test of the series.

The pitch at Madras was somewhat under-prepared and the

ball was spinning after tea on the first day. After a long
partnership by Shoaib and Javed we lost some quick wickets,
and were then 247 for 5 at the end of the first day. Then I made
my third Test century and took Pakistan to a total of 487. This
long innings on a slow spinning wicket set up my batting for
the rest of the series. However, when I bowled in India's first
innings I couldn't get any kind of rhythm. The wicket was
under-prepared, the run-up soft and sandy. Because of my
jump, I need a good foothold, and in India there was no grip in
the landing area. I couldn't find my rhythm, and lost pace and
accuracy, and produced some of the worst bowling of my
career. Our bowlers made very little impression on the Indian
batting in their first innings at Madras. They scored over 500,
and the match petered out in a draw with the third innings of
the match only half over.

After the first Test we realised that we would be playing
most of the tour under such conditions, and that the Indian
attack would rely mainly on the two left-arm spinners, Maninder Singh and Ravi Shastri. Javed Miandad suggested that it
would be a good move to call up Younis Ahmed, who was a
left-hander and a good player of spin bowling, to counter the
threat posed by the Indian spinners. I asked the Board to send
him, and he joined us before the second Test. He had not
played Test cricket for more than seventeen years and was not
included in the team for the second Test, since it was the only
one likely to be played on a pitch that promised to be of
assistance to seam bowlers. However, Kapil Dev didn't have
sufficient confidence in India's vaunted batting line-up, and the
pitch was shorn on the eve of the Test.

We won the toss and put India in to bat, because this was the
only way we could hope to bowl them out twice. I knew that
although the grass had been cut, this was the best track for fast
bowling we would encounter throughout the tour. We had
them in some trouble at 149 for 5, and then Azharuddin and
Kapil Dev both played good innings and took India beyond
400. On the one pitch with a relatively firm surface, I bowled
extremely badly and took 0 for 93 in India's first innings.

Our reply began well, but we progressed too slowly against the Indian spinners and made 46 in 26 overs before lunch on the third day. By the time India took the second new ball after tea, we had reached only 170. For some reason the second new ball was really seaming on the evening of the third day. Binny put in an inspired spell of seam bowling, taking 4 for 9 in 30 balls after tea, and we were in danger of having to follow on. Salim Yousuf played a determined innings of 33 and got us out of a corner. When India batted again on the fourth morning they had a lead of 174. Strangely, after Srikkanth was out relatively early on, they made little attempt to push the pace and leave themselves sufficient time to bowl us out again. I was somewhat surprised by these tactics and I think we were lucky to save the match in the end.

Realising that we were going to play the last three Tests on a succession of slow, spinning pitches, I called for reinforcements. Iqbal Qasim, the orthodox left-arm spinner, joined us and played in the third Test, as did Younis Ahmed. India batted first at Jaipur, making the worst possible start when I had Gavaskar caught at slip off the first ball of the match. The pitch was easy-paced, and the rest of the batting did not have much trouble on it: India again scored over 400 in two full days.

When we arrived for play on the scheduled third day, which followed the rest day, we found that overnight rain had seeped under the covers. There were patches on one side of the pitch just on a good length for a left-arm spinner. The Indian cricket authorities wanted us to play, but the umpires agreed with us that the pitch was unplayable and not fit to be played on according to the rule whereby it has to be in the same condition as it was at the close of play on the day before. On the fourth day the umpires were overruled and the match restarted on a pitch that had not yet recovered sufficiently. The administrators did not want to make it obvious that the covering facilities were not up to Test standard. We made a written protest but it was overruled. There was nothing more we could do, because General Zia-ul-Haq was visiting Jaipur as part of his 'cricket diplomacy' – an attempt to defuse tension between the two countries. For some reason, Kapil Dev chose to bat on for a couple of overs before declaring. I suppose he wanted to prove that the pitch was perfectly all right. We lost two quick wickets and then Rameez and Javed, with sound and patient defence, righted matters. Luckily for us Maninder wasn't playing, and India's two off-spinners, Shivlal Yadav and Gopal Sharma, and the left-armer, Shastri, were unable to exploit the conditions. By the end of the fourth day we were 228 for 6 and still needed 38 runs to save the follow-on, which we did fairly easily next day. I continued to bat well, making 66.

Tauseef Ahmed and Javed Miandad were both unfit and did not play in the fourth Test at Ahmedabad. Ijaz Faqih, another reinforcement, was included in the team. Everyone was expecting a turning pitch that would crumble, but the Ahmedabad wicket turned out to be another slow turner. We batted first and scored only 130 runs on the first day. Rizwan-uz-Zaman and Younis were almost strokeless for hours on end. At 167 for 6 on the second day our situation didn't look too good until Ijaz Faqih and I set up a seventh-wicket partnership of 163. Ijaz went on to make a century in his third Test, and I made 72. He played the spinners with confidence and never allowed them to pin him down. India in their turn also played cautiously, reaching 165 for 3 at stumps on the third day. The Ahmedabad crowd was fiercely anti-Pakistani throughout the match. On the fourth day some of the Pakistan fielders were stoned and I had to take the team off the field. We were able to resume play after a seventy-minute stoppage only because the Pakistani deep fielders put on helmets to protect themselves against stone-throwing by the crowd.

It had been a dull, uninspiring series so far. After the fourth Test, Kapil Dev issued a statement blaming me for negative cricket and for the lack of interest in the series. His statement annoyed me immensely. It was clear that we were not at fault either for the boring and tedious series of draws or for the general disenchantment of the public. India, who had the advantage of playing at home, had chosen to make pitches on which exciting cricket was just not possible. If they were unwilling to take chances when conditions favoured them, I was certainly not going to oblige them by taking the initiative. As I mentioned earlier, Kapil Dev had specifically asked the groundsmen to cut the grass of the pitch at Calcutta. He was content to play a waiting cat-and-mouse game, thinking that at some point our inexperienced side would crack, and was unwilling to take any risks to force the issue. He chose to release a statement attacking me so as to defend himself against criticism of the Indian team's inability to beat us in spite of their alleged superiority.

By this time the public was screaming for results, and everyone knew that the pitch at Bangalore would be a genuine turner. Qadir had been out of form throughout the tour and his confidence was low, so, despite the wicket, I chose not to include him, and we went into the match with three seamers and only two spinners. Had Ijaz Faqih been fit, he would have played again in place of Salim Jaffer. At a team meeting before the game I told the players that only one side had played under pressure during the series, and that the Indian batsmen had never been in a difficult situation in the previous Test matches. I told them that this was to our advantage and that if we didn't panic we could win the match. We won the toss and after a dozen overs the Indian spinners were on: the ball was turning square before lunch on the first day. Our middle order made the mistake of going for their shots in an attempt to get runs before they got out. This was an unwise tactic on a pitch that required application and the slow accumulation of runs. We were all out for 116, and by the end of the day India had made 68 for 2 in reply. On the second day they passed our first-innings total for the loss of only four wickets, but then proceeded to make exactly the same mistakes as we had committed.

Vengsarkar, who was batting well and had made 50, played a strange attacking stroke and was caught. The rest of the batsmen followed him to the pavilion in a similar fashion and India were all out for 145, only 29 runs ahead. They had

1. The first Test at Edgbaston, 1982. I was caught off this attempt to hook Bob Willis. This was my first Test as captain, and I realised that if I was going to lead by example I would have to cut out this kind of shot. I ended the series averaging 53

2. David Gower superbly caught by Wasim Bari

3. On my way to 65 in the second innings

4, 5. After the last Test at Headingley, 1982. Although I was
pleased to be made Man of the Series I was disappointed we'd
lost 2-1. The name 'Lion of Pakistan' was invented by our
supporters in England, and only appeared in Pakistan after the
1982 series

6, 7, 8, 9. Abdul Qadir is a great bowler and an essential part of
the team. This sequence shows his action and one that beat
Botham, Wasim Bari and first slip during the second Test at
Lord's, 1982

10, 11. *Above:* setting the field with Qadir. *Below,* umpires
often give batsmen the benefit of the doubt, as here in the second
Test at Lord's, 1982

12. Some other important Pakistan cricket contemporaries. *Above,* with Zaheer and Qadir. My T-shirt was the creation of Kerry Packer's marketing people

13, 14. *Below left:* with Sarfraz.
Right: Majid Khan

15, 16, 17. *Above left:* Mushtaq Mohammad. *Right:* Javed
Miandad. *Below:* Asif Iqbal

18. The Karachi Test against India in 1982: Sarfraz congratulates
me on my 200th Test wicket during a spell of 8 for 24

certainly let us off the hook by their purposeless batting. To take some of the pressure off the team, I told the players before we began our second innings that I didn't care if we won or lost as long as every player went out there determined not to sell his wicket cheaply, and this was exactly what happened. Everyone fought, and each batsman had to be prised out. Rameez Raja and Salim Malik scored 47 and 33 respectively, after which each player played above himself. I got 39, Salim Yousuf made his usual plucky contribution, and Iqbal Qasim, whom I promoted to the middle order because he was a left-hander, managed 26. As our score grew, the pressure on the Indian spinners mounted. Every run mattered on a pitch like this, and any inaccuracy on their part yielded vital runs. Having an extra spinner didn't really help them as Kapil, in an attempt to get quick wickets, was bowling the three spinners in rotation and every change led to a few more runs as the new bowler settled down. It was spinning and bouncing so much that it was hard to bowl on.

India had to make 221 to win the match. Wasim Akram gave us just the start we needed, taking two early wickets with his version of the fast leg-break. We knew that the only obstacle between us and victory was Sunil Gavaskar. On the fourth day we worked our way slowly through the Indian batting, but he kept up one end with a display of controlled, organised batting. He countered the spin by playing the ball very late. Tauseef and Qasim were magnificent and bowled unchanged throughout the day. Qasim's experience was a great asset.

I found this the most difficult match I have ever had to captain. I knew I shouldn't say anything discouraging to the spinners, because any critical comments would merely have put more pressure on them. The fielders were very tense and, with marginal decisions going against us, I knew I had to keep calm. If I showed any anger, the entire team's nervous energy might spill over and we would lose the match. When Qasim finally dismissed Gavaskar for a brilliant 96 we knew the match was over. A few late blows from Binny were like the death throes of a landed fish. We won the match by 16 runs and took the series 1-0.

The fifth Test was a nail-biter from start to finish – a dream Test match. The tensions of a great Test are of a different order from those of any other game, or the instant excitement of one-day cricket. It is unique because it is a complex, subtle story that develops over five days and, like great fiction, encompasses many moods and situations. After a Test match like that at Bangalore the rest of the tour was bound to be an anti-climax.

We annihilated a depressed Indian team in the one-day matches and then returned home to the sort of reception that makes a whole career worthwhile. The crowd that came to welcome us at Lahore stretched from the airport to the heart of the city. It took us hours to wend our way home through a singing, dancing multitude of over 200,000 that lined the roads in celebration of Pakistan's first victory over India on their soil. But another first remained to be accomplished – beating England in England. After what we had just achieved, anything seemed possible.

CHAPTER 7

England in 1987, and
the World Cup

At the press conference which was held immediately after our arrival in England, I sensed a general disbelief and scorn when I said that we could win. England were riding high after their victory over Australia and in three one-day tournaments. We were thought of as a stepping-stone on the way to their cricketing glory. We were treated with disdain by the Test and County Cricket Board, the press and even the Customs from the moment we arrived. At Heathrow the team was made to stand aside, while other passengers looked on, as sniffer-dogs went through our luggage.

We started the tour badly when Kent beat us by an innings. Javed and Qadir had still not joined us for personal reasons – Qadir because his wife was ill, Javed because he was trying to release his car from Customs. I missed the first two games because I was mentally and physically exhausted and wanted to recuperate, and I had started a course of light weight-training on nautilus machines to build myself up, having lost half a stone on the Indian tour. All the same, I played in the third match against the reigning county champions, Essex. Graham Gooch got a 'pair' in the match, which we won by an innings. It was the worst summer in years and many matches were rained off, a thoroughly inadequate preparation for the Tests to come. Most of the players were on their first tour of England and desperately needed to acclimatise themselves to English conditions. To add to our problems, Salim Jaffer, our third fast bowler, had still not recovered from a groin injury. Javed Miandad joined us just in time for the one-day internationals.

We went into the one-day series as complete underdogs. We were thrashed in the first game and I was extremely irritated when at the post-match press conference an English journalist asked me whether things had gone as I had expected. We won the next one-day game rather easily and would have won the third but for some excellent hitting by DeFreitas at the end of the match.

In the pre-tour meeting with the TCCB we had expressed our reservations about David Constant's umpiring, and asked that he be appointed for only one Test, if at all. We felt that this would create a better atmosphere in the series. We pointed out that India had objected to Constant on their previous tour, and that he had been withdrawn from the Test series. The TCCB was adamant, saying that their umpires were the best and they had complete faith in them: they then leaked details of this confidential meeting to the press, which attacked us immediately – a journalist actually rang me up to tell me to apologise to David Constant. After the third one-day international, the tabloid press virtually accused us of cheating. Mohsin Kamal and Mudassar Nazar, both of whom had developed injuries during the match, had gone off the field after completing their quota of overs. They quoted Mike Gatting and Micky Stewart as suggesting that this was part of a conscious plan to substitute good, fresh fielders for poor ones. This was obviously nonsense, since Mudassar was one of our better fielders, but this sort of accusation was to become a regular feature of the tour. The press quickly jumped in, and very soon our team had become the target of irresponsible criticism.

By the second Test match we were fed up and our manager, Haseeb Ahsan, counter-attacked. An outspoken and extremely patriotic man, he is not someone to take things lying down. Nor was he the kind of subservient *Kala sahib* or anglophile manager from the sub-continent that the English cricket administration were used to dealing with, and they were somewhat surprised by his combativeness. The English press retaliated by characterising him as a bumbling, ill-spoken, coarse sub-continental – a character out of a Peter Sellers movie, the sort who spoke bad English and bungled everything. The press was so derogatory in its attacks on Haseeb that even some Pakistanis became embarrassed. Unfortunately some of us still see ourselves through the eyes of our erstwhile masters. Haseeb has made many mistakes and has not always acted in the best interests of Pakistani cricket, but on this tour he was doing his job as he saw best.

We were happy to get the first two Tests out of the way. The first Test was at Old Trafford. The pitch looked damp, and I put England in to bat: I had pulled a stomach muscle and was not fully fit, so I thought that our best chance was to bowl them out on a helpful wicket. However, we didn't bowl at all well and they notched up a high score. Our batting failed, and without Mansoor Akhtar's accomplished innings of 75 we might not have reached three figures. The rest of the match was rained off.

The second Test at Lord's was also curtailed by rain. Qadir had arrived, and played at Lord's, but he made little impression on an easy pitch and looked out of form. England batted first and made 368 before the rain took over.

We went into the third Test at Headingley still missing two of our key players, Rameez Raja and Salim Jaffer. England won the toss and batted first on a bright sunny morning, the kind of day on which Pakistan play their best cricket. I was fully fit again, and attacked the English batting on a pitch which had little bounce but plenty of movement. Wasim Akram and Mohsin Kamal gave me good support and England collapsed to 31 for 5, eventually struggling to a total of 136. We had them in a corner, and our batting continued the good work. Foster bowled magnificently, but Botham was injured and Dilley and Capel didn't use the conditions well. This was the match in which Salim Malik came of age as a Test batsman. He held the innings together with a display of resolute and disciplined batting, scoring 99 in five and a half hours. Late hitting by Ijaz Ahmed and Wasim Akram took our score to 353.

England began their second innings 217 runs behind. By the end of the third day they were 186 for 7 and the match was won. I used all my experience, varying pace and strategy, sensing that this was my chance to fulfil my ambition of beating England in England, and I took 5 for 38 in 17 overs. Next day we wrapped up the England innings to go one up in the series, and I finished with 7 for 40. The roles had been reversed.

The fourth Test was played at Edgbaston on an easy-paced pitch. We batted first and Mudassar made a cool, efficient century. Then Dilley ripped the heart out of our batting order, reducing us from 284 for 3 to 289 for 6 in seventeen deliveries. Salim Yousuf then took on the England bowlers. Supported by the tail, he made 91 not out and we topped 400. England batted and got even more. Although I took six wickets, Qadir was ineffective, because the pitch had no bounce at all and he was still bowling below his best. We went in to bat again after tea on the evening of the fourth day, and were 38 for no wicket at the close of play.

Edgbaston is an easy pitch to bat on until the clouds come over, and it was ominously cloudy on the final morning. At lunch we were 79 for 1 and looked pretty safe. But for some reason I felt uneasy, and I decided to leave the stadium for the nets. I got some useful practice there, because Neil Foster produced a superb spell of controlled seam bowling and dismissed Shoaib, Mansoor and Javed in quick succession, while Botham accounted for Salim Malik. At 144 for 6 we were only 62 ahead, with a good deal of time remaining. A few runs later Ijaz had also gone. Yousuf stayed with me through fourteen overs, until he holed out at short cover just before tea. Now every minute and every run counted. Wasim Akram didn't last long but Qadir and I hung on through ten overs. Then Foster, the man of the hour, trapped me l.b.w. and brilliantly ran out Qadir. We were all out for 205, and England's victory target was 124 in eighteen overs.

Before going out to field I thought we had very little chance of saving the match, and soon my worst fears were confirmed.

Broad gave England a scintillating start, and with England's professional approach and one-day experience, it seemed that they would easily get there. Edgbaston has such a large outfield that they only needed to place the ball around, getting singles and the occasional boundary. After nine overs, England were 62 for 3 – halfway there, with nine overs to go. We were defending desperately, throwing ourselves all over the field in a forlorn attempt to save the match. Then England, for no good reason, lost their way. They started taking unnecessary risks and did not follow the basic principles of one-day cricket. For some strange reason they played like amateurs, trying to blast their way to victory rather than approach their target methodically. They failed by nine runs.

By the fifth Test at The Oval, most of the team felt that Qadir was out of form and should be dropped. I didn't agree. I knew that the wickets so far had not really suited his bowling and that the pitch at The Oval, which had a little more bounce, would help him. In addition, I regarded Qadir as a match-winner and would always play him unless there were good reasons for not doing so. The Oval proved to be a good batting pitch on which the ball came on to the bat. We batted well, and England's attack looked toothless without Foster, who by now was a spent force at the end of a long season. He is an honest pace bowler who gives his all, whether in a Test or a county match. Javed Miandad was in his element and made a massive 260. Salim Malik and I contributed centuries and our total reached the stratosphere. Long before we were all out for 708 the series was over and we knew that we had become the first Pakistani side to win a series in England.

When England came in to bat Qadir proceeded to show why he is one of the great spinners of modern times. On a pitch with some bounce and a little bit of turn he took 7 for 96 as England were dismissed for 232. When England followed on, Qadir struck again and England were 95 for 3 at the end of the fourth day, still 381 behind.

The last day of the match was one of those days when nothing went right for us. We missed countless chances and allowed Gatting and Botham to bat out almost the entire day to save the match. We had won the series, but with all the carping England had done throughout the summer, I was a bit disappointed that we didn't win the series 2-0. However, this was just a passing thought. The main thing was that we had won, and in a matter of a few months we had beaten India and England on their home grounds. My two main ambitions had been fulfilled. The World Cup was still to come: I certainly wanted to win, but Test cricket had always meant much more to me, and the World Cup could only be the icing on the cake.

England lost the series for a number of reasons. To begin with, they had an inflated opinion of their strength, which made them too complacent. When we arrived I told them that we were a team to be taken seriously but they paid no attention. In Australia they had won easily and had never been under any pressure. They had the strange notion that they could beat us easily. The fact is that they didn't have many outstanding players in their side and were quite beatable. They made some very odd selections throughout the tour, leaving out match-winning batsmen like Graham Gooch and Allan Lamb. I would have persisted with Gooch, even though he was out of form at the start of the season. Without Lamb and Gooch, their top order had a somewhat defensive look. Then they went into matches with only two frontline seamers, plus Botham. Botham was no longer the bowler he had been, and they should certainly have played a fourth seamer instead of persisting with two spinners against batsmen who played spin very well and had had plenty of experience in India just a few months earlier. Neil Foster had to carry too heavy a workload, and by the fifth Test it was obvious that he was suffering. Surprisingly, England didn't include seamers like Radford or Jarvis or DeFreitas in their team. In the final analysis England were beaten by a side that was better and more motivated on the day. The most amazing comment from a Test captain was Gatting's statement at the end of the tour that he thought England had won the series on points.

The 1987 World Cup proved to be the most colourful and exciting to date. Pakistan were the favourites before it began, but I was not all that optimistic. I knew we had a good chance, but one-day cricket is so unpredictable that anything could happen. I was not pleased with the team's performance in the first match against Sri Lanka. The fielding was extremely sloppy and the bowlers looked out of form: we came pretty close to losing the match. Then the team pulled off two amazing victories against England and the West Indies in quick succession. We had come together again. I thought that we had the most varied bowling attack in the World Cup and we batted right down the order.

After the group matches our fans had begun to believe that the World Cup was already Pakistan's. I knew we had a long way to go, but it looked as though an already *unstoppable* twelve months was going to be capped with the World Cup. But one-day cricket is a lottery: on any given day a team can pull off an upset, and Australia proceeded to do just that in the semi-final.

It was a match in which everything went wrong, and the day was a complete nightmare. Mudassar pulled out of the team in the morning with a stiff neck and we had to include the out-of-form Mansoor Akhtar. Apart from our missing Mudassar's bowling and his experience, Mansoor was under a good deal of pressure from the press and was not really in the right frame of mind. Australia won the toss and batted, and we produced our worst bowling performance in eighteen months. Our bowling had recently been our strong point, but that day for some reason it just didn't click. Wasim Akram and Salim Jaffer, who had served us well so far, bowled poorly, well below their potential. Our fielding – which was always a worry – was also poor, and an injury to the wicket-keeper, Salim Yousuf, proved very expensive. Javed Miandad tried his best, but Salim's absence from the field cost us at least 15 or 20 runs and one vital catch.

Even though Australia had put up a large total I thought we still had a chance of winning the match. The Australian bowling was not particularly strong and was pretty straight-forward, and they didn't have anyone who could really trouble us. But we made the worst possible start: Rameez Raja, our most successful batsman in the tournament, was run out in the very first over, and then Mansoor, under pressure, played a really bad shot. But the greatest blow was the dismissal of Salim Malik, who had been in great form and was the batsman I thought most likely to win us the match. Javed and I then proceeded to repair the early damage, and did so quite com-petently. To begin with it made sense for us not to lose wickets, but then we needed to push on. I felt that if anyone could do it, Javed could, for he was our star batsman. But his innings was somewhat awkward, so I felt I should try to take the initiative. I got the scoring rate moving but he seemed unable to acceler-ate – which I found hard to understand, because he is such a good player of spin bowling and such an improviser. I don't know what happened to him. Maybe he was just too tired because of having to keep wicket. In the end, our tail-enders had too much to do.

The way we played the match, we deserved to lose. I felt particularly annoyed at losing in that, although we played our worst cricket in all three aspects of the game – batting, bowling and fielding – and although the Australians excelled them-selves, there was a difference of only eighteen runs at the end, and we undoubtedly had the better team. On the day we let ourselves down. Although I felt pretty bad about it, my own ambitions were never centred on one-day cricket, and I knew that the best team doesn't always win. The most obvious example of this was the 1983 World Cup, when the best team, the West Indies, lost to India. The West Indian team of that time was, in my view, the best in history. They had batting, bowling and fielding strengths, and for them to lose to India – who were subsequently soundly thrashed by the West Indies in India – proves that, in one-day cricket, upsets can always happen. From the public's point of view it would have been great to have won the World Cup: the whole country was solidly behind the team, and that was the saddest aspect of our defeat. I have never seen the Pakistani public so disappointed as they were after our semi-final defeat. I had underestimated the depth of feeling about the World Cup: most of the people leaving the stadium had tears in their eyes.

CHAPTER 8

All-Rounder

Until 1982 my history as an all-rounder was rather confused. At school I had started off as a batsman, and had no interest in bowling – as far as I was concerned it was something which had to be done in the nets to give the others a chance to bat. Eventually I bowled a bit because I found that fielding for hours was rather boring, but all my ambitions were concentrated on batting.

My interest in bowling began in the school nets, when I happened to be listening and watching while our coach, Aslam Khokhar, showed one of the other boys how to hold the ball for an outswinger. Instead of bowling aimlessly in the nets, I started trying to swing the ball as I had seen it done, and after a few days I began to have some success. Eventually I could bowl outswingers quite reasonably, but my bowling was still confined to the nets.

At the same time – I was then about fourteen or fifteen – I suddenly shot up about three inches, and this extra height helped my bowling enough for me to be allowed to bowl for the school. Although wayward, I managed to work up a reasonable pace, and got the outswinger going. Between the ages of sixteen and eighteen, my bowling took over from my batting: my ambitions had not changed – I still wanted to become a batsman – but, because of the standard of pace bowling in Lahore and Pakistan, it was the easiest way to make progress. There was abundant batting talent, and my batting was not considered good enough anyway.

So I made my first-class debut for Lahore as an opening

bowler, after having earlier represented the Lahore under-nineteen side. When I was sixteen I discovered that I wasn't strong enough for first-class cricket, and I pulled a back muscle, which troubled me for a whole year. A cousin told me I should do some back exercises, so I stopped bowling for a month or two and built up my back muscles.

When I came back, I found that I had lost the outswinger, and was now bowling inswingers. I think I'd been putting too much pressure on my back trying to bowl outswingers, and without knowing it I had become more chest-on, encouraging the inswinger. In fact, this was no bad thing, in Lahore cricket at least, because the inswinger was more effective in getting wickets, especially against the late-order batsmen, whose poorer technique was shown up.

Even so, when I played my first Test for Pakistan, in 1971, I reckoned that, like Asif Iqbal and Majid, I would eventually become a batsman. I still had no real ambitions as a bowler. At about that time my cousin, Javed Burki, asked Khalid 'Billy' Ibadulla to come and look at me in the nets. Ibadulla took one look at my bowling action and said that it was a 'young man's' action, and that I shouldn't expect to bowl for very long.

At Oxford I was considered a batting all-rounder, and Colin Cowdrey once told me during a match in the Parks that I should concentrate on my batting. This backed up what Aslam Khokhar had always told me, and I had the school batting records to prove it.

Until the winter of 1975–6 I was a medium-pace swing bowler. Then I went back to Pakistan, and my bowling started to change. For a start, I had to bowl much more, and my pace increased: I also realised that merely bowling inswingers was never going to get me anywhere in Test cricket.

Back at Worcester in 1976 I continued to be thought of as a batsman who could bowl a bit, and I still thought of bowling as something to stave off boredom. As soon as I did well as a batsman, I would not take my bowling seriously any more. But I began to find that whenever there was a chance of a result, or a tense situation, my bowling got quicker and better. For the

95

first time I began to realise that I could become a *fast* bowler, and from then on my interest in bowling revived. I began to think of myself as a strike bowler who could win matches for Pakistan.

After the Test win at Sydney in January 1977, when I took 12 wickets, I never looked back as far as bowling was concerned, and for the first time batting became secondary. I started working on my bowling action, increasing my training, and trying to build up particular muscles. I did more press-ups, for my shoulders, and I started running more, for my legs.

Although I still enjoyed batting, I could no longer afford to pay as much attention to it, and it had to suffer. My bowling improved consistently until the 1982–3 series against India, when the stress fracture appeared. Each season added something to my bowling, and I worked at my action and run-up with the help of Mike Procter, John Snow and others. Geoff Arnold played briefly for Sussex, and he helped me as well. Meanwhile I experimented continuously in county cricket – bowling round the wicket, trying to get closer to the stumps, trying to get more side-on, trying out the leg-cutter. The closer I got to the stumps, the more effective the inswinger seemed to become, and by the time of that fateful 1982–3 series, I felt that everything had fallen into place. I picked up 40 wickets against what was perhaps the best batting line-up in the world, and on some of the easiest pitches for batting.

As for batting, in some ways I was unfortunate in being an opener in the early part of my career at school. I went on to play club cricket as an opening batsman, and made my first-class debut as such. As a result, my approach was that of an opener, and it was on that basis that I knew how to build an innings. Suddenly I found myself playing for Pakistan and batting at eight or nine in the order, and I did not know how to play down there. Either I found myself slogging, if we had made a lot of runs, or I had to defend in a crisis, not knowing which shots to play. I was completely at sea, and even now I sometimes come across other early-order batsmen with similar problems if they have to come in some way down the order.

Only when I first played for Oxford University did I begin to bat properly. I was promoted to number four, and gained a lot of valuable experience. Once the Oxford season was over, I had to return to Worcestershire, where I went back to number seven, and found it impossible to score any runs. The number seven in county cricket is usually batting when the team is in trouble on a greenish or spinning pitch, or he has to go out and hit for bonus points.

In 1976, I asked Worcestershire's captain, Norman Gifford, to put me at number four. In the first match, I scored 143 against Warwickshire, so I stayed at number four and had my best-ever season for Worcester. When I got back to Pakistan I was down at eight or nine, and once again I found it difficult to build an innings and felt obliged to hit out when the tail-enders came in. It wasn't until I became captain of Pakistan in 1982 that I realised that to start slogging when the tail-enders come in is about the worst thing you can do.

In my first season for Sussex, in 1977, I found myself down at number seven again, and hardly scored a run. Next year I batted higher in the order and scored much more consistently.

On tour for Pakistan I found it hard to concentrate on my batting as I was considered a strike bowler. I hardly got any batting practice in the nets, and when I did it was against irregular bowlers who were not much good. As the team's main bowler, I was often rested from the side games on tour and missed the chance of more practice, so I was rarely in top batting form for the Tests.

My other batting problem is with my top-hand grip. Because of an injury I sustained when I was only five, my left arm – which was broken and dislocated, and never set properly – does not extend to its full length. As a result my top hand is weaker, and the muscle there tires quickly. Unless I bat consistently and give it regular exercise, I soon lose the full use of the muscles in the left hand: I cannot grip the bat properly, and this in turn affects my timing. I have to have special handles on my bats to offset the problems caused by my weak left arm and peculiar top-hand grip. All this means that if I don't practise regularly and have a bat with a special handle, I can't time the ball well or bat properly.

My batting at Test level improved after I became captain, since I felt that I had to set an example to the rest of the team. Even when batting at number seven, I had to bat as an opening batsman, not giving my wicket away. Once I was batting better, I felt I was in a position to criticise the others if they played bad shots.

My batting improved further after I broke my leg and had to play solely as a batsman for two years. I played two one-day series, including a World Cup, and half a Test series just as a batsman, and my batting got better by leaps and bounds. I realised that I could have been an even better batsman if I'd been able to concentrate on it earlier. I think I did the best batting of my career in India in 1987, when I nearly always had to bat in some sort of crisis. However, I have no regrets about the way my career turned out. My one disappointment is that on the Pakistani wickets my all-round performance was hampered, because the pitches were such that bowling was extremely difficult. They were basically dead pitches, which were very good to bat on, but because I was bowling so much I never got the opportunity to do so properly. Moreover, at number seven – apart from against the West Indies – I had few opportunities to bat since Pakistan rarely had to bat twice at home.

When people talk about career averages and run aggregates, I think more attention should be paid to where the runs were scored, against what calibre of opposition and at what stage in a player's career. I played very little Test cricket while I was at my peak: there were long periods when I played nothing but first-class cricket. On the other hand, Botham had the opportunity of playing regular Test cricket, five matches at home and then five or six matches abroad. It is easier to run up impressive performances if you are playing regular Test cricket while you are at your peak.

The hardest thing of all is to become a fast-bowling all-rounder. You have to put in a lot of training to be able to bowl

Opposite: 1. Emma Sergeant's portrait of me, painted while I was recovering from the stress fracture

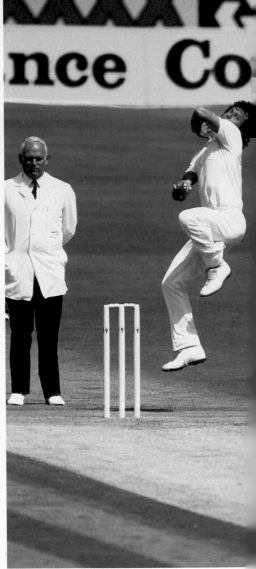

2, 3, 4, 5. My action has developed a great deal since the 1970s. Thanks to help from Mike Procter and John Snow, among others, it's been getting better and better throughout the 1980s. This sequence of one delivery was taken in the third Test against England at Headingley in 1987

fast; the bowling itself is very tiring; in whatever time is left over you have to work on your batting and fielding. When I used to have nets at the Lahore Gymkhana, I wondered why I seemed to have to work so much harder than the others – especially when it was boiling hot! Wasim Raja and Talaat Ali, both of whom also went on to play for Pakistan, also had nets there at the same time: not only did they hardly have to work at all, but they went out and scored runs with great fluency while I was struggling. I used to feel quite downcast after working so hard while they hardly seemed to have to bother. I suppose in the end the hard work pays off.

At that time we didn't have any fast bowlers in Pakistan, so I used to get strange looks when I was working out. I remember running round the Bagh-i-Jinnah ground at Lahore, and people stopped and stared at this mad guy running around in the hot weather.

I often used to find when I was playing for Pakistan that I was too exhausted to bat properly, because we frequently went in to matches with only two pace bowlers – Sarfraz and myself – and sometimes no more than three regular bowlers. Against the West Indies at Karachi in 1980–1, I opened the bowling with Iqbal Qasim, a left-arm spinner. I found it difficult to go in to bat and concentrate hard if I had just bowled a long spell, often in hot weather. At Perth in 1981–2 I bowled 29 overs on the first day, then bowled unchanged as we got Australia out on the second morning. Our batting then collapsed, and I had to go in about twenty minutes before lunch. I was so tired that when I stretched forward I had cramps in my hips. Needless to say I didn't last very long, and we were all out for 62 – after which I had to bowl 39 overs in their second innings!

However, I think I've been lucky compared to a lot of other players, in that I am naturally physically fit, and this has enabled me to do reasonably well at batting and bowling over the years. I know a lot of players who might have become all-rounders but chose to concentrate on one aspect of their game. From the Pakistan team, both Sarfraz and Qadir could have become fine all-rounders, but concentrated on bowling

Opposite: 6. Directing net practice during the Benson and Hedges Perth Challenge in 1987

only: even so, Sarfraz eventually passed 1000 runs in Tests, and Qadir may well do so before he retires.

Comparing all-rounders is a difficult business. Just because a player can both bat and bowl, he can't necessarily be compared to another player who is also described as an all-rounder. Even comparing batsmen is difficult. Take Viv Richards and Sunil Gavaskar. Both are batsmen, but there the similarity ends – their styles are as different as chalk and cheese. It is doubly difficult to compare all-rounders. I am often likened to Ian Botham, but in fact he is a completely different sort of player: he is an aggressive batsman, whereas I try to build an innings; I am a fast inswing bowler, and he is – or was originally – a medium-pace outswinger.

Botham made his Test debut in 1977, whereas I made mine in 1971, yet he has played many more Tests than I have. The same goes for Kapil Dev, who first played in Tests in 1978–9 but has already played about ninety matches. The all-rounders I think of as being closest to myself are Richard Hadlee, who made his Test debut at about the same time as I did, and his former Nottinghamshire colleague Clive Rice.

Hadlee has played his Test cricket for New Zealand, which – like Pakistan – has always been short of fast bowlers. Like me, he has often been a lone spearhead for his country and, like mine, his opportunities for playing Test cricket have been limited by the fact that New Zealand doesn't play many five- or six-Test series. Over the years Hadlee has perfected his control to such an extent that he is probably the most dangerous bowler on a greentop that there has ever been. He has cut his run-up without losing much pace, and his outswingers can be almost unplayable.

There can be no higher praise than to say that Hadlee bears comparison with Dennis Lillee. Both usually made the ball leave the right-hander, and both were blessed with classical, smooth, side-on actions which enabled them to bowl for long spells over a period of years. Hadlee, of course, was almost unplayable in county cricket – he was particularly difficult to deal with at Trent Bridge, where the pitches proved to be ideal for him, offering a little bit of bounce and some movement off the wicket. But I haven't found him that effective on Pakistan pitches – in fact he did not tour with New Zealand on their last visit. In his native New Zealand, of course, he has had a lot of success – the pitches there also encourage movement off the wicket – and he has also done phenomenally well in Australia on their often bouncier tracks.

The one criticism I've heard of Hadlee is that he sometimes becomes defensive when a batsman attacks him. Instead of taking up the challenge, he tends to go into his shell and bowl defensively. There was an example of this at The Oval in 1986, when Botham was on the rampage – he eventually reached 50 in 32 balls – and Hadlee, with the new ball, spread the fielders all round the field and bowled line and length stuff. I also was told by the West Indians that when Hadlee toured the Caribbean, he was not the same attacking bowler they feared from county cricket.

Hadlee and I have a lot in common as bowlers, both in approach and background, but our batting styles are worlds apart. When Hadlee has a good day with the bat, he can be devastating; otherwise the bowler always feels he has a chance. On the other hand, he must be one of the best bowlers of all time. For match after match, for many years now, he has been responsible for carrying the New Zealand attack.

Ian Botham is more of a gambler. He is not a machine-like bowler like Hadlee, but relies more on surprise and on taking risks – and in the process he can often prove to be very expensive. He takes a lot of chances, and is at his best when his team have scored a lot of runs and he can buy a few wickets. Unfortunately, in situations such as England found themselves in against the West Indies under David Gower, Botham becomes a liability because he gives away so many runs. Nevertheless, he has confounded the critics over the years and keeps on getting wickets.

When he started off Botham was a much better bowler than he is now. He was a yard or so quicker, and he had a wonderful outswinger. Now, for some reason, he has just about lost the outswinger. This may well be because he has put on weight, which makes it more difficult for him to get side-on, but it could also be due to the change in cricket balls after 1981. The balls which were used in English cricket before 1981 favoured swing bowling: since the regulation changing their make-up, Botham's usefulness as a bowler has declined.

As a batsman, Botham is easily the hardest hitter of the ball in world cricket. He is immensely strong, and has shown time and time again that he is prepared to hit the ball for miles. He also hits it very cleanly, and with excellent timing. His batting is at its most dangerous when there is nothing to lose, as against Australia in 1981, when England seemed to be in a completely hopeless situation. Poor Kim Hughes, the Australian captain, failed to realise that Botham would continue to hit out: he could easily have put everyone on the boundary and cut off most of the big hits, but instead he continued attacking, and Botham kept on smashing the ball over the top.

Occasionally Botham has changed his approach and has played a sensible, controlled innings, most notably against Pakistan at The Oval in 1987, when he and Gatting batted almost throughout the final day to save the match. He also played a very responsible innings of 69 against us at Lord's in 1982. However, especially when he was captain, he seemed unable to control his instinct for long enough to be able to set an example to the others.

Botham's consistent failure against the West Indies counts against his batting record. In seventeen Tests he has not scored a century and, compared to his record in other Tests, his average is very poor.

I find Kapil Dev and Ian Botham similar in many ways. Both started off as bowlers who could bat a bit, but as they went on their bowling, instead of improving like Hadlee's or mine, became less effective. In Kapil's case, his decline may well be the result of bowling a lot on the unhelpful Indian pitches. He has also suffered a knee injury, which has reduced his pace and effectiveness in recent years; and he has had an enormous workload, often playing not one Test series a year but two or three. When Pakistan arrived in India for a five-match series in 1986–7, India had already played three-Test rubbers against Australia and Sri Lanka.

Another problem for Kapil Dev is that he has often been the only pace bowler of any quality in the Indian team. He has not won many Tests outside India, though he has always been effective, if not devastating; yet I find him one of the most intelligent bowlers in the world cricket, and someone who always seems to be bowling to a plan. Like Botham's, his batting seems to improve when he is not the captain. He's at his most dangerous when he can go out and play his own game without worrying too much about the demands of captaincy. Now that he is no longer in charge I'll be interested to see how he performs. During his captaincy, the only time he played a controlled innings was against us at Calcutta early in 1987, when India were in a lot of trouble in their first innings.

Because of South Africa's international isolation, Clive Rice has not had the recognition he deserves. I have always had a high regard for him as an all-rounder and feel that, of all the players I have mentioned, he is the most similar to me: he is an upright, orthodox batsman and was a fast bowler in his younger days, though he tended to seam the ball rather than swing it. Before his neck injury, Rice could bowl as quickly as anyone. His approach was simple: to hit the seam and bowl fast. He was also a very solid batsman, with a good temperament, and an intelligent captain. I found him rather vulnerable to short-pitched bowling, because he tended to favour the front foot too much. He had a rather peculiar grip on the bat, not unlike Glenn Turner's, which made it difficult for him to pull or hook; but he could drive with great power, and was a tremendous player in the 'V'.

Clive Rice is a great competitor who fights very hard, and I am sure he would have succeeded in Test cricket if he'd been allowed to play. The pressures in Test cricket are quite different from those of county cricket, but Rice was highly thought-of in World Series Cricket, and I can see no reason why he would not have succeeded at the highest level.

The other South African all-rounder whom I rated very highly was Mike Procter, another great competitor. He was a very powerful hitter, and could destroy spin or medium-pace bowling. He too was a little suspect against short-pitched bowling. Had he been able to play more Test cricket he might have learned to cope with it, but there weren't many fast bowlers in county cricket when he was playing. He didn't get bounced much in South Africa because he was able to dish out some mean bouncers of his own in return. As a bowler he was fast and adventurous, a risk-taker who relied on inswing as well as the useful bouncer. By the time I played with him in World Series Cricket his knee injuries had reduced him to a medium-pacer, but he was still a very competitive cricketer indeed.

The all-rounder who towered above us all was Garry Sobers. He could do everything: if he wasn't batting or bowling fast, he was bowling spin or taking incredible catches. Sadly, I never saw him in his prime, but I have heard tales about him and, by all accounts, he was the greatest. In his day he could play an innings of pure genius: even Sir Donald Bradman rated his 254 at Melbourne in 1971–2 against Lillee the most outstanding he had ever seen. In that innings Sobers was out for revenge, because Lillee had shot out his World XI at Perth and dismissed him for a duck in the first innings. In the second innings Sobers cut loose: Lillee went for 133 in 30 overs, while O'Keeffe, a useful leg-spinner, bowled 27 overs for 121. Sobers played him like a medium-pacer and smashed him all round the Melbourne Cricket Ground.

Sobers would take on a challenge, and that's what makes him the best in my book. And he could bowl: apparently on his day he could be as quick as anyone. He was brilliant when people needed him. In the day-in, day-out requirements of county cricket Sobers was not too bothered, and rarely rose to such heights. I only bowled to him once, when I was about twenty and he was playing for Nottinghamshire against

Worcester. I was bowling outswingers, and he was playing the ball so late that I often thought I'd beaten the bat, but he hit every one in the middle. That was his hallmark – he had more time than other batsmen. Even when I pitched the ball up to him, he played it late off the back foot.

Because of the decline of spinners, or rather the recent ascendancy of pace bowlers, there have not been many spinner all-rounders in recent years. Mushtaq Mohammad could have become an outstanding all-rounder, a batsman-cum-spinner, but he never bowled enough – especially in Tests, where he was hampered by the presence of Intikhab Alam. Intikhab himself was a fine leg-spinner and a useful batsman, though he never developed his batting enough. Ravi Shastri might develop into a genuine all-rounder, but he is not really outstanding in either department at the moment.

Abdul Qadir could easily have become a genuine all-rounder, in that he had a lot of ability as a batsman. When inspired and motivated, he has played some vital innings for Pakistan, and he could have made a top-order Test batsman if he had worked hard enough at it. But some bowlers don't want the pressure of batting as well. This strikes me as a cop-out, which forces the specialist batsmen to take all the pressure.

Mudassar Nazar could be described as an all-rounder. His bowling is much better than people think. Had he been English, he would undoubtedly have made his mark as an even more valuable all-rounder, but unfortunately his kind of medium-pace bowling is not suited to the pitches in Pakistan. Mudassar proved almost unplayable at Lord's in 1982 during his 'golden arm' spell of 6 for 32.

I have a great deal of faith in Wasim Akram. I think he will become a great all-rounder, as long as he realises how much hard work is required. His batting needs attention, but he has the advantage of thinking like a lower-order batsman: he doesn't have the problems of being a frustrated opening bat. As a bowler he is extremely gifted, and has it in him to be the best left-armer since Alan Davidson. He is the one genuine swing bowler among the current crop of Test cricketers.

Steve Waugh may well develop into a good all-rounder, and will certainly be an important one for Australia. He made his debut for New South Wales while I was playing for them. Bob Radford, the secretary of the New South Wales Cricket Association, made him share a room with me for away matches so that he could learn from me, but Waugh kept so quiet that I thought he was suffering from lockjaw. Although he never said a word, I could tell that he was ambitious and fiercely competitive. His rapid rise since then has shown that he does indeed have the right temperament. He is a talented batsman, and could become a useful Test bowler. But, like all the others, he will have to remember that to become a Test all-rounder you have to put in probably twice as much work as other cricketers.

It was only through hard work that I achieved my ambition of being the best all-rounder in the world. In two series in England I was made man of the series ahead of Ian Botham, and in two out of three series in India I received the same award. In fact during the third series, when Kapil Dev won it, I was suffering from an injury.

CHAPTER 9

Best of the Rest

As far as I am concerned, the sign of an outstanding player is his ability to perform well consistently under pressure. He must also be a complete team man.

The bowler who really stands out is Dennis Lillee, and I had the great fortune to play against him when he was at his best, in 1976–7, on my first trip to Australia.

The first Test was played on a very slow pitch at Adelaide, and I was immediately impressed by Lillee, who kept on bowling long spells even though he was getting nothing out of the wicket. Early on he lost his opening partner, Jeff Thomson, who injured himself in the field, and from then on he had to carry the attack. When he realised that there was no alternative but for him to keep bowling, he cut his run-up and started varying his pace: he would try anything to take wickets. In the second innings of that match he bowled nearly fifty eight-ball overs, taking 5 for 163. I thought very highly of his single-minded attitude: he was always attacking, and trying to think of ways to get the batsman out.

The next Test was played at Melbourne. By the end of the first day I felt depressed in that I had bowled really badly on a helpful pitch. Conditions were excellent for swing bowling, and there was some moisture and movement off the seam as well, yet I had sprayed the ball all over the place. Australia eventually scored 517 for 8, with Greg Chappell and Gary Cosier making centuries, and I ended up taking no wickets for 115 from 22 unimpressive overs. Lillee sensed my dejection, and came over to speak to me afterwards. To my surprise he sympathised with me: he realised that whereas I had bowled at Adelaide on an unhelpful pitch, this time I had got excited at seeing the ball moving about and had tried to do too much. It's a mistake that many young fast bowlers make, and it was encouraging that someone like Lillee should come over and discuss the problem. After this we became good friends, and I began to bowl better as well: in the final Test at Sydney I took 12 wickets and we won the match.

I don't think that Lillee was as much of a natural athlete as some of the other great fast bowlers of my time, like Thomson, Holding or Marshall. He has a much stronger physique than the others, but he was not as loose-limbed, and he had to work to keep fit. When I first saw him on television in 1972, his action was that of a real tearaway fast bowler – it was uncontrolled, and you could tell that he was putting immense strain on his body. Not surprisingly, he soon went down with an injury, which turned out to be a stress fracture in his back. This threatened to end his career, but he fought back, remodelled his action and, through sheer guts and determination, became an even greater bowler. I can probably appreciate the problems he faced better than most people, because of suffering a similar stress injury later in my career.

Lillee's greatest asset was that he would rise to the occasion, especially in front of those huge crowds at the Melbourne Cricket Ground, getting life out of the dreadful pitches they had there at the time. His determination showed through against Pakistan at Sydney in 1972–3, when there was obviously something seriously wrong with his back: he insisted on bowling, and – off a short run, and backed up by the inexperienced Max Walker – bowled Pakistan out when we looked like winning. Most other bowlers in this situation would have given up, and his refusal to do so makes Lillee number one in my book.

The other great fast bowler of my time was Jamaica's Michael Holding. I've never seen a more gifted bowler. He was a natural athlete, and possessed a perfect bowling action. Once he had cut down his run he was able to bowl for long spells without taking too much out of himself. He could do every-thing with the ball: he could swing it, he could move it off the pitch, and he could obtain awkward bounce from well pitched-up deliveries.

Holding provided the fastest bowling I've ever seen during a World Series Cup match at the Sydney Showgrounds. It was a one-day match, and Sarfraz and I, playing for the World XI, had bowled the West Indies out for about a hundred. Some rain then affected the pitch slightly: luckily for us, it also reduced our victory target to about 70. Holding ran in from one end and Roberts bowled from the other, and it was the only time I ever saw batsmen trying to get away from the strike at one end so they could face Roberts, who was also in his prime. Holding was bowling like the wind: when I went in to bat, the wicket-keeper, Deryck Murray, was standing so far back that I couldn't see how the ball could possibly reach him. Whenever I see Desmond Haynes, I remind him of that spell. He remembers it well: he was fielding at short leg, and he had to shout to Murray to make himself heard, because the keeper was so far away.

I saw Holding subsequently bowl a couple of spells which approached the pace of that day at Sydney, but they were on the fast pitch at the WACA at Perth. His most famous spell was at The Oval in 1976, when he bowled England out twice on a very slow pitch of the kind on which England should have survived easily. But Holding beat them through the air with sheer speed, taking 8 for 92 and 6 for 57. Nine of the batsmen were bowled and three were l.b.w., which gives some idea of his pace during that match. I find it hard to believe that anyone has ever been quicker than Holding at his fastest.

Holding's only problem was a result of his being so naturally gifted: he did not have to put in that much work, and may not have been as fit as he should have been. Quite often he broke down with injuries, one of which led to his retiring from Test cricket at the age of thirty-three. I suspect that if he had really worked at his fitness he could still be bowling fast in Test matches.

109

Another fast bowler who deserves to be called great is Holding's former partner, Andy Roberts. I first saw him when he came down to Oxford with the MCC. He was playing for Hampshire's second eleven at the time. When our turn came to bat, we wondered what on earth was going on: Oxford had just beaten Northants in the Benson and Hedges Cup, and we thought we were playing well, but we couldn't lay a bat on this unknown fast bowler. Perhaps – we thought – we had celebrated our B&H win too well! But as the season wore on, we started to notice the Hampshire second eleven's matches in the small print of the newspapers: their opponents kept declaring at about 60 for 7, after Andy had put two or three players in hospital.

Roberts really emerged in the following year, 1974. He was genuinely fast, and it was the first time for years that county cricket had had such a quick bowler. He was out to prove himself, and he terrorised a lot of county batsmen with his change of pace and two ferocious bouncers – one obvious one, and the other concealed, which took the batsmen unawares. I learned about his bouncers the hard way. I hadn't worked out why he hit so many batsmen, and I was facing him in a one-day international at Berbice, in Guyana. Pakistan had been struggling, but then Asif Iqbal and I had a bit of a partnership, and were starting to hit out in the closing overs. Roberts came on, and I hit him back over his head for four. I was prepared for a retaliatory bouncer, and I was rather surprised to see him amble up to the crease rather than run in hard. This put me off my guard, and I didn't expect to see him bowl a bouncer. Of course, he did – and I didn't see the ball until it was about two feet away from my face. In a reflex action I used the bat to protect my face, and the pace of the ball was such that it flew out of the ground for six. I was quite pleased with the shot, and told everyone that it was intentional. In fact I was petrified at the time, and if the ball had hit me it might have ended my career.

Later on in that 1976–7 series, I faced Roberts again, this time at Kingston. Since I knew he was going to bounce me I had given him a few of my own when he was batting, so I was expecting a warm reception. As luck would have it, I went out while Roberts was in the middle of a fast spell, and he bowled me the quickest ball I have ever faced – the one I described earlier, which had kissed my cap and passed the wicket-keeper, Murray, by the time I was halfway through my shot.

Contrary to popular opinion, Roberts was a very intelligent bowler. He was a good reader of the game, and probably the first West Indian fast bowler who thought hard about thinking out the batsmen. He passed on his knowledge to a later generation of West Indian quick bowlers, all of whom became excellent bowlers, using their brains as well as their brawn. Roberts had a big hand in the West Indian revival of the 1970s.

Joel Garner made his Test debut against us in 1976–7. When I first saw him I thought he couldn't possibly bowl fast or accurately from such a great height, and that he would soon fade away. Little did I know that here was one of the greats. On his day he could bowl as fast as anyone and was probably the most accurate paceman of recent years. He didn't do a lot with the ball, but with his great height he could extract a steep bounce, and he had a well-concealed change of pace. He often had to perform the role of stock bowler for the West Indies, while Holding and Roberts were resting; and he had been the strike bowler more often he would probably have taken even more wickets. In any event, his record stands comparison with the best.

Colin Croft also made his Test debut against us, at the same time as Garner, and he was genuinely fast. He was also genuinely nasty as a fast bowler, and could sustain his pace for long spells. His bouncers could be positively dangerous. He didn't seem to enjoy playing cricket very much, and often looked miserable when playing county cricket for Lancashire. His career was not a long one: in the end he opted for the big money and went to South Africa.

A bowler who should have made a name for himself in international cricket was Sylvester Clarke. Once again, I never felt he was particularly interested in the game. He had an awkward bowling action, but he could bowl very fast at times. He too had a very fast, swinging bouncer, and could be very unpleasant to face. Like Roberts, he terrorised county batsmen for a time. I didn't see enough of him in Test cricket to judge his temperament at the highest level, but he certainly produced the goods in county cricket. People often accused him of throwing, but I'm not sure about that. Had he not been West Indian he would almost certainly have made his name playing for another country.

The best fast bowler around at the moment is another West Indian, Malcolm Marshall. I was not impressed the first time I saw him playing for Hampshire: he was inaccurate and didn't do too much with the ball. Perhaps it was Andy Roberts's tutorship again, but he became a great fast bowler very quickly. He has learned a lot in county cricket: his main weapon is an unusual skidding bouncer, which does not get up much but keeps coming at the batsman, who often finds it difficult to get underneath it.

Marshall has an unorthodox action, not particularly side-on. He relies on the strength of his legs to sprint up to the wicket, after which he rushes quickly through his action, which provides him with his pace. He doesn't swing the ball, but moves it about a bit off the pitch. He is an intelligent bowler who quickly assesses a batsman's weaknesses. He is also a natural athlete – it must be very difficult to sustain pace with that action. The best spell I saw from him came against Australia at Adelaide in 1984–5. The other West Indian pace bowlers were struggling a bit with injuries, and on a pitch that was not offering much help he twice ran through the Australian batting, taking 10 wickets in the match.

I rate John Snow most highly among English fast bowlers. Unfortunately I never saw him at his best – for example, on England's tour of Australia in 1970–1, when he took lots of wickets – and by the time I was playing in England he was having trouble with the administrators. He didn't pull out all the stops when playing for Sussex, but he needed inspiration: once motivated, he was a fine bowler. In many ways he was a similar type of bowler to me: our stock balls came in to the right-hander, although I swing it in and he relied more on movement off the pitch. He also had a good leg-cutter, a difficult ball to master. I had a lot of respect for Snow: he understood bowling and taught me a lot.

In terms of figures, Bob Willis is one of the best fast bowlers England has ever produced, but his performances outside England were not that great. I am most impressed by those who can shine on all pitches, in any part of the world, so I can't rate him at the top, but he was genuinely fast on occasions. His performance at Leeds in 1981, when he took 8 for 43 and shot out Australia for 111, is one of the greatest and most memorable spells of fast bowling of my time.

Jeff Thomson would be many people's choice as the fastest bowler of recent years, though I would go for Holding. Thomson was capable of producing a blindingly fast delivery from his slinging action, but he relied on sheer pace and quick wickets to really shake up the batsmen. Unfortunately, the first time I saw him, at Adelaide in 1976–7, he dislocated his shoulder early on, and although he occasionally came up with a fast spell afterwards, he never seemed as effective. Viv Richards in particular took him on once or twice and hit him all over the place. He relied too much on pace, lacked control and didn't move the ball. On tour in Pakistan in 1982–3 he was almost ineffective on the slow pitches, picking up only three wickets in the three Tests.

During my career there have been very few outstanding spinners. From time to time someone does well on a helpful pitch, but on ordinary wickets most of them fall onto the defensive. The exception, of course, is Abdul Qadir, who must be classed as an attacking spinner. Qadir is in a class of his own: Richie Benaud, who is no bad judge of a leg-spinner, told me in 1983 that Qadir was the most talented bowler he had seen for twenty years.

Qadir undoubtedly has problems with his temperament at times. He can let things get on top of him, and if he's hit about you can see him going downhill and losing control. Recently, though, his attitude had improved, and he has become an even better bowler for it. His greatness lies in his control and his variety. He is not usually a great spinner of the ball, but he has immense variety and can bowl two types of googly, one that is obvious to the batsman and one that often beats the wicket-keeper as well. He has also perfected the flipper, though it does not bring him as many wickets as it should. Outside Pakistan in particular, umpires often fail to understand the mechanics of the flipper, which in effect acts like the off-spinner's arm ball.

As we have seen, I insisted on having Qadir in the team when I became captain of Pakistan. I thought this was an attacking move, going against the normal role of spinners nowadays, when they are often used in a defensive role unless the match is being played on a helpful pitch. None of the other spinners around today could be described as an attacking bowler, though Maninder Singh of India might eventually become one.

I remember being quite astonished when Abdul Qadir told me the story of his early life. His father was a *maulvi* or mullah, whose income of 120 rupees a month – about £4 – had to support a large family. At times the family could hardly afford bread. As a youngster, Qadir often woke at four in the morning, went to the local market at Sabzi Mandi and bought vegetables to sell in his own area before going to school. He also had to work after school to supplement the family income. His interest in cricket was entirely self-generated: he played in the streets and on vacant plots of land, wherever and whenever he could find a game. Unable to afford proper trousers, he played in *shalwar kameez*, the native dress of a long flowing shirt and baggy pantaloons. As he got better he became known as the hard-hitting batsman who always wore *shalwar kameez*. When he eventually acquired a pair of trousers he had to hide them because he was afraid his father would dis-approve, so he took them to the ground and changed there. His career has had its ups and downs, and he has been dropped for long periods because the selectors have not appreciated the value of his rare art.

The story of off-spinner Tauseef Ahmed's entry into Test cricket is equally fantastic, every schoolboy's wildest fantasy come true. In 1979–80 the Australians toured Pakistan for a three-Test series under Greg Chappell, with Border, Hughes, Lillee, Marsh and the rest in the team. Despite the presence of Sarfraz and myself in the Pakistan side, the strategy was to produce turning pitches which would blunt the threat of Lillee. At that time we had only one spinner of note – Iqbal Qasim, an orthodox left-arm bowler. The twelve for the first Test at Karachi had already been named, and included an off-spinner who had performed well during our first-class season.

During practice, a friend of Sarfraz's and mine mentioned a lad who had bowled devastatingly in a local league. We didn't take him seriously, because we knew the quality of the pitches on which these local matches were played. Our friend insisted that we give this off-spinner a try, so, just to humour him, we agreed. Next day Tauseef came to the nets and, after watching him for an hour, we realised that he was indeed better than the team member who had been originally selected. So Tauseef, who had never been near anything resembling a Test match, was drafted into the side. He had a match analysis of 7 for 126 off 64.2 overs, and his victims included Kim Hughes (twice) and Greg Chappell. He proved to be the perfect foil for Iqbal Qasim, and we won by seven wickets.

The two other great spin bowlers I have played against were Bishan Bedi of India and Derek Underwood of England, both left-armers but with very different styles. Bedi had a wonderful flight, which stemmed from an easy, classical, side-on action. He could bowl for hours and spin the ball even on the slowest pitches. Sadly, when I played against him he was past his best: and he also came up against Zaheer in full flow, a daunting prospect on the easy-paced Pakistan pitches.

I was always very impressed by Derek Underwood, who not only had immense control but a surprising amount of variety. He bowled at almost medium pace, and although he was not as dangerous as Bedi on good pitches, he was lethal on helpful wickets. I have never seen anyone as dangerous as Underwood on damp wickets: not for nothing was he known as 'Deadly'. Once the water had got under the covers at Lord's in 1974 he brushed aside our batting, taking 8 for 51 in the second innings. We were not happy about the covers proving faulty, but were saved from defeat by more rain, which washed out the last day's play.

Where batsmen are concerned, Vivian Richards stands head and shoulders above everyone else. His greatness lies not only in his talent, but also in his determination. He has immense pride in himself and his team. He has the best reflexes of any batsman I have come across. When I first played against him, in the West Indies, I was not a genuine fast bowler, but I did vary my pace a bit. He played me almost as if I were a spinner: to block my inswing he would put his front foot down and across the wicket. I would continue at medium pace and then try to surprise him with a bouncer: although he was on the front foot he would merely lean back and hit the ball over mid-wicket. I had a recurring nightmare on that West Indies tour – that Viv and I were two Wild West gunslingers, and had to draw against each other. In dreams you are slow anyway, and it is not hard to imagine how I felt trying to outdraw Viv Richards.

Richards has had a great deal to do with the West Indies' supremacy over the years. He has gone out against fast bowlers like Lillee and Thomson, and has not just tried to stay there but has gone for them and knocked them about as though he was playing in a school match. This attitude makes it much easier for the following batsmen, who realise that the bowlers are only human: and the bowlers' confidence is shattered when their best deliveries are carted about. I remember an innings Richards played against England at Trent Bridge in 1980. He came in when Greenidge had scored about 4 or 5: not long afterwards Richards was out for 64, by which time Greenidge had moved on to 6 or 7. I asked Richards afterwards if he had got something against Bob Willis, because he had been especially hard on Willis's bowling. Richards replied that when he was younger Willis had come out to the Caribbean with England. He had hooked him once, but was out the second time he tried it, and called Richards a 'black bastard' as he walked off; Richards was always keen for revenge. He continued where he had left off, and in 1984 smashed Willis about again and virtually ended his Test career. Richards has great pride in his race and colour, and is not one of those apologetic West Indians who try to behave like Englishmen. He is capable of rising to the big occasion: think of all those runs he has scored in big finals at Lord's, or the huge crowds at the Melbourne Cricket Ground in Australia.

I was amazed when Somerset sacked Richards, because he had always tried his utmost for the county. Somerset were struggling because they had a poor team, with no one to back up Richards and Garner. They did all right in one-day matches, but in the championship you need good back-up bowlers. Take Hampshire, for example: Malcolm Marshall has done consistently well for them in recent years, but because their other bowlers are not penetrative enough they've never won the championship in that time.

Gordon Greenidge is another West Indian who has impressed me greatly over the years. He is an exceptional batsman who can defend if he needs to, but when he attacks he's as good as anybody. He has played two outstanding innings against Pakistan, the first in Jamaica in 1976–7, when he scored 100. Only Collis King, who slogged 41, got more than 34. Greenidge's innings was a mixture of watchful defence and blistering attack. Then, at Lahore in 1986–7, he scored a very patient 75 to set up West Indies' win. Apart from Richards, who made 44, none of the others reached 20, but Greenidge brought all his experience to bear, exercising great restraint. This was the match in which we were shot out for 77, allowing the West Indies to square the series after our win at Faisalabad. They got their revenge for Qadir bowling them out for 53 in the first Test.

Greenidge's main problem is that he seems very injury-prone. He is often seen limping about at the crease, yet in some ways he then seems to become even more dangerous. I have never seen anyone score as many runs while apparently injured. He can play well off both feet, and cuts with ferocious power. He is one of the most complete batsmen I have ever seen.

Surprisingly, Greenidge's record in Australia is not that great, though he has done consistently well in England, especially in Tests: who will ever forget his double-century on the last day of the 1984 Lord's Test? England had set the West Indies a stiff target, but Greenidge made it look silly with a tremendous innings, and the West Indies reached 344 for 1 to win with about an hour to spare.

The other outstanding West Indian batsman of my time is, of course, Clive Lloyd. I found it easier to bowl to Lloyd than to Richards or Greenidge because my natural delivery was going away from him. But he has a tremendous Test record, and he nearly always got runs for the West Indies when they were most needed. He was still batting well when he retired, and the West Indies have not yet found an adequate replacement for him. Lloyd was a very hard hitter of the ball, usually off the front foot. Like South Africa's Graeme Pollock, he used a very heavy bat, so if he hit anything more than a yard or so away from a fielder you could usually give it away and watch the boundaries mount up.

A player who was coming to the end of his career as I began mine was Roy Fredericks, the West Indian opener. A wristy left-hander, he was another fine timer of the ball. I didn't see much of him, although on the West Indies' 1976 tour of England he seemed to be an exciting batsman. His great innings was his 169 at Perth in 1975–6, which was remarkable by all accounts. He reached his hundred in just seventy-one balls, hitting 27 fours and a six in all against Lillee and Thomson at their peak. Lloyd also hit a hundred in this match, which the West Indies won by an innings.

It's hard to compare the merits of Pakistani batsmen. We have had a lot of talented batsmen over the years who might be termed 'great', but to some extent the measure of their greatness must depend on their opportunities to perform in Tests while at their peak. For instance, Mushtaq Mohammad played most of his first-class cricket in the 1960s, when Pakistan played hardly any Tests, but a lot of so-called unofficial Tests against touring elevens from many countries. On the other hand, Javed Miandad played his first Test in 1976–7, since when Pakistan have played an almost non-stop series of Tests and one-day internationals.

From 1972 to 1976–7 Majid Khan was easily the best batsman in the Pakistan team. He had so much time to play the ball that he hardly needed any footwork and relied on his reflexes and his good eye. Later in his career he began to struggle because his reflexes became a bit slower and he did not have the footwork or defence to compensate. Even at his best he had the occasional bad patch and could look ordinary, but when he struck form he was marvellous. One of his best innings anywhere came in 1974, when he hit 109 in the one-day international at Trent Bridge. He dispatched an experienced England attack – Willis, Peter Lever, Old, Underwood and Greig – all over the ground. Majid also scored a century before lunch against New Zealand in 1976–7 – one of only four batsmen to do so on the first day in a Test. This outstanding innings not only demoralised the bowlers, but gave Javed the chance to score 206 at the age of nineteen.

In 1974 Majid saw off Bob Willis, who was then bowling at his fastest: he also dealt admirably with Lillee and Roberts when they were at top speed. His hook shot was a treat to watch: only Viv Richards plays this shot better than Majid at his best. Unfortunately, when we came home after the West Indies tour in 1977, Majid was tired and took seven months off from cricket (he had already stopped playing county cricket for Glamorgan). He was never the same batsman after that. He went straight on to World Series Cricket, where there were no easy matches in which to sort out your form, and where he kept coming up against fast bowlers like Lillee, Pascoe and all the West Indians.

Majid had a problem in regaining his form, but he felt sure

that he would soon be all right again. He didn't want to retire from cricket on a disappointing note, so he hung around, waiting for a good series so that he could go out with a bang. Sadly, that good series never came, and he eventually left cricket feeling rather embittered.

Another great Pakistani batsman was Asif Iqbal. He emerged at about the same time as Majid – in fact they opened the bowling together in their first Test in 1964–5 – and for some years he was considered a medium-pace bowler who could bat a bit. He scored a memorable century for Pakistan at The Oval in 1967, and eventually his batting progressed to the point where he hardly bowled at all.

His trademark was his quick footwork, which seemed to get him into position more quickly than other batsmen. He had all the strokes, some of them unorthodox, though by the end of his career he had become much more selective. He was a great batsman with the tail-enders: he seemed to organise things so well. He was also very quick between the wickets, which meant that he could steal the strike almost at will.

I remember batting with Asif during World Series Cricket for the World XI against the West Indies. We needed about 250 to win and were 90 for 6 when I came in. Thanks to Asif we won the match. For most of the time I was an admiring spectator at the other end: the West Indies were quite unable to stop the flow of runs. Rather surprisingly, he was generally considered one of the best batsmen in World Series Cricket. The Australians, however, were not too surprised after Asif's efforts in 1976–7: in the first Test at Adelaide he scored 152 not out, adding 87 for the tenth wicket with Iqbal Qasim, who made 4. He also hit 120 in the third Test, which we won.

Sadly for Pakistan, Asif Iqbal became a great batsman at a late stage of his career, when he had worked out which strokes were profitable. He was a complete team man, and never played for his average. Unfortunately, when he was just about at his peak, he was appointed captain for our disastrous tour of India in 1979–80, after which he felt compelled to retire even though he was still a class batsman.

Statistically one of Pakistan's all-time greats, Zaheer Abbas was certainly the best timer of the ball I have ever seen. There may have been harder hitters, but no one could match his timing. At Karachi in 1982–3, during his 186, he went to drive a ball from Kapil Dev and found that it wasn't quite up to him. He checked his shot and played defensively, and his innate timing sent the ball away for four past cover. The cricket commentators kept replaying this shot on television, pointing out that Zaheer hadn't even followed through. His exquisite timing meant that he was a great player of spin bowling, which he could take apart on good batting pitches.

Zaheer could play off either foot, and through either side of the wicket, but his main problem was one of temperament. As soon as he was under pressure he found it hard going, and often fell into a bad patch. Once in a run of poor form, he often found it difficult to break out again.

He also had a problem with pace bowling. It didn't seem to worry him early in his career, but in the early 1980s he suffered a form of shellshock. He was never the same after Sylvester Clarke had hit him on the head during the West Indies tour of Pakistan in 1980–1, often making excuses or taking the easy option by hitting out wildly against the slower bowlers. He was also very conscious of his average, which counts against him in my view. I can't really rate him in the top flight of batsmen.

Even so, Zaheer was one of the best one-day cricketers I have seen, and his excellent timing often produced runs against tightly set fields. Although Javed Miandad is a much better player under pressure, it was always noticeable that if he and Zaheer were batting together and in form, Zaheer would easily outscore him. One of the best partnerships I ever saw was put together by Majid and Zaheer against the West Indies at Georgetown in 1976–7. Zaheer replaced Sadiq, who had retired hurt, and the pair took the West Indian bowlers apart. Majid made 167, one of his greatest innings, and Zaheer, who at that stage was not worried by quick bowling, scored 80. They added 159 in two and a half hours. They shared a similar partnership against the same opposition in the 1979 World Cup semi-final at The Oval. They put on 166 and it looked as though they had set up a Pakistan victory, but sadly the rest of us could not carry on the good work.

Javed Miandad is currently the best batsman in our team, and he is already the most successful batsman for Pakistan in terms of runs scored in Tests. I find it hard to say whether he is the greatest-ever Pakistani batsman: everyone who saw Hanif Mohammad bat rates him very highly, and he carried the Pakistan batting for years, as the only batsman of any class.

There is no doubt that Javed is our top batsman now. He is a real street-fighter, and the displays he sometimes puts on are an indication of his competitiveness. He learned his cricket in a hard school, and he always tries, whatever the importance of the fixture. I ran some six-a-side matches for my benefit in 1987, and found it difficult to get involved with this sort of knockabout cricket, but Javed was always in there, fighting like a tiger.

In Mianwali, my father's village, one of the local axioms is that 'the status of a man is measured by the status of his enemy'. I was brought up with that ideal in mind, and I have always found it difficult to perform my best when the opposition is not very good. When Sri Lanka came to Pakistan in 1985–6, we won quite easily, and I found it hard to motivate myself. But Javed has no such problems, and he took the opportunity to score another double-century at the Sri Lankans' expense.

Javed is an excellent player of spin bowling, even on bad pitches. He likes taking risks and loves to improvise. He has played some good innings against the faster bowlers, but his technique against pace may be a bit suspect. He gets very square-on, and is often trapped l.b.w. I think Javed needs to score more runs outside Pakistan to be rated as great. So far his main scores have come in Pakistan, and they have helped him maintain his excellent Test average. He did score a tremendous 260 at The Oval in 1987, but that was his first Test century in

England. My main criticism concerns his fielding. At first I thought he was the best fielder in the world, that anywhere in the field he would be outstanding. As I have often told him, his fielding has declined markedly, which is sad to see in someone so young.

Last but not least among the Pakistanis is Mudassar Nazar. He deserves a special mention, because although he does not measure up to the other greats he has achieved a lot in Tests through sheer hard work. He is a very intelligent player, and uses his cricket brain to the full: he has worked on his batting technique, and has tried hard to eliminate any faults. He is also a more than useful change bowler. As a batsman, he will best be remembered for a phenomenal series against India in 1982–3, when he scored 761 runs in the series, with innings of 119, 231, 152 not out and 152. During his double-century he shared a Test record stand of 451 with Javed.

Moving over the border to India, it will come as no great surprise if the first name I select is that of Sunil Gavaskar. His record is such that he must remain one of the all-time greats. Gavaskar has had a great influence on Indian cricket, matched in recent years only by Kapil Dev, whose main significance was that of being the first bowler of any pace that India had produced for many years. But Gavaskar has made the greater contribution in my opinion. In the 1950s and 1960s Indian batsmen had a reputation for avoiding fast bowling, and some of them were known to back away towards square leg if a quick bowler came on. Gavaskar changed all this. He played pace with relative ease: he could hook if he wanted to, but more often he would leave the bouncer alone and watch it sail by. His defence is well organised, and he is a very intelligent batsman who performs well under pressure. Indeed, he has played some of his best innings under intense pressure: twice India has made a good fist of chasing over 400 to win a Test, and on both occasions Gavaskar was the major factor. Against the West Indies in Port of Spain in 1975–6, Gavaskar scored 102 to set his side on the way to 406 for 4, the highest score ever made to win a Test. And at The Oval in 1979 he hit a magnificent 221 as India chased 438. They fell a few runs short of improving their record, but drew the match.

The best innings I ever saw him play was his 96 at Bangalore, in what turned out to be his final Test. It was one of the most difficult pitches I have ever seen – the ball was turning square, bouncing awkwardly and sometimes keeping low. Pakistan were bowled out for 116 in the first innings, after which India made 145. Thanks to gritty play by our tail-enders, we set India 221 to win, and Gavaskar played an incredible innings. Both teams knew that the match would be over if Gavaskar was out, which is what eventually happened: Iqbal Qasim had him caught, just short of what would have been his thirty-fifth Test century.

He is the master of an unusual shot: a type of late flick which he plays with great control between square leg or mid-wicket. I have never seen any other batsman play this shot with such precision. It brings him a lot of runs, which is one reason why he can keep his score ticking over. Although he has had to cut out a lot of his more risky shots in the team's interest, he can be brilliant when he lets himself go, and I have seen him outscore stroke-makers like Srikkanth on occasions.

I batted with him for a long time during the MCC bicentenary match at Lord's in 1987. He scored 188, I made 82, and we put on 180 for the fifth wicket. I found it a revelation to see how he tackled certain bowlers, and how he understood the game. He is a master, and I am afraid that Indian cricket will struggle to replace him adequately.

Another Indian batsman whom I rate very highly is Mohinder Amarnath. He seems to be something of an enigma: I have rarely seen such a classy batsman, yet he has been in and out of the Indian Test team. He has suffered some severe head injuries against the fast bowlers, but he keeps coming back. As far as I'm concerned, he should have been playing for India non-stop since his debut in 1969.

He ducked into a bouncer in 1978–9, yet he came back and played reasonably well in the second innings. In the next Test he played some incredible shots and showed no sign of any ill-effects from the blow on the head. He really hammered the West Indies in 1982–3, scoring 58 and 117 at Port-of-Spain, 54 and 116 in Antigua, and 91 and 80 at Bridgetown. While making his 80 he was hit on the face early on by Malcolm Marshall, yet he came back and continued his innings. I spoke to Marshall about it, and he said he couldn't believe the shots Amarnath played after being hit. Yet the following year the West Indies toured India, and Amarnath couldn't get a run. In three Tests he scored 1, and five noughts, which included two 'pairs'. But still he comes back, and after missing the 1987 World Cup he was brought back by India to face the West Indies again. Had I been his captain I would never have dispensed with him – he's a player on whom you can depend when the going gets tough.

India's new captain, Dilip Vengsarkar, has been a very consistent batsman over the years, but he's not in the same league as Gavaskar or Amarnath. He is very effective, especially on the on side, but he sometimes looks a little awkward, falling over to the off when he is batting. He has a good temperament, though occasionally in the past he has played for himself rather than the team. It will be interesting to see how he does as captain.

The English batsman who I considered to be world class was Geoff Boycott. My first encounter with him was in 1974 at the Parks, when he was captaining Yorkshire. As the Oxford captain I went to him for the toss. I was immediately struck by his arrogance. Instead of using my name he called me 'young man', and even felt it unnecessary to go out into the middle to toss the coin. His whole attitude made me feel small. He won the toss and – rather to our surprise – put us in. Some of the Yorkshire boys told me later that he didn't want his customary century against a university team to be affected by a bit of morning moisture.

We were bowled out quickly. When he went in to bat, I tried to bowl as fast as I could and got thrashed for my pains. When play began the next day he had reached the 60s. For an hour I bowled one of my best spells of medium-paced inswingers at

Oxford, and finally got him out, 13 short of his century, with the perfect inswinger. It gave me more satisfaction that any other delivery during my Oxford days.

Subsequently his attitude changed towards me; in general one only gains respect in sport through one's ability. He even gave me a valuable piece of advice in Australia before the 1976 Sydney Test match, emphasising the importance of bowling flat out with the new ball on hard wickets – unlike in England, where one has to bowl line and length.

But that first encounter at the Parks gave an indication of his character. He was extremely self-centred. No matter what the match, he ruthlessly wanted to score runs, and he carried a huge chip about Oxbridge players. He was certainly not a modest man either. I once heard him on the radio, and he was asked to name the best opening bat produced by England. Well, he said, two immediately sprang to mind – Hutton and himself.

He wanted to captain England, as a result of which he sometimes refused to play for England under Denness and Greig. Being so self-absorbed, he was totally unsuitable for the job even though he had a fine understanding of the game.

He captained as he batted, never taking risks. But, even though as a batsman he played for himself, he was a great player in Test matches. His technique was watertight and his concentration almost incredible. He would never give away his wicket, no matter what the situation. Later in his career, when he was a little shaky against fast bowlers, he would still fight it out. In the 1980–1 Caribbean tour of the West Indies, he performed better than all the other English batsmen, despite being well past his prime.

I have always thought Ian Chappell the best Australian batsman I ever saw. Again, he was a man for a crisis, a great player of both pace and spin. He often got runs for Australia when they needed them: the greater the challenge, the greater he became.

Greg Chappell also comes into the 'great' category, although he was a different type of player from his brother. He was a very correct batsman, his strength lying in his driving and his ability to play in the 'V'. Occasionally he would run into trouble against short-pitched bowling, the result of his predominantly front-foot technique. He scored a great many runs against Pakistan, hitting 235 at Faisalabad in 1979–80 and 201 at Brisbane in 1981–2. He bowed out of Test cricket with a fine innings of 182 against us at Sydney in 1983–4.

Allan Border also merits consideration as one of the modern greats. He has scored runs everywhere in the world and has made many of them under extreme pressure, often looking the only player of any class in the team. He has a very commendable temperament, and always seems unruffled in times of crisis. Like Greg Chappell, he seems to enjoy our bowling: against Pakistan at Lahore in 1979–80 he got 150 not out in the first innings and 153 in the second, a Test record.

Barry Richards and Graeme Pollock were the two great South African batsmen of my time. I didn't see a lot of either of them, but I saw enough of Barry Richards to tell that he was a fine player. He was never off balance when playing his shots, and his technique seemed watertight. It was a shame that he never played much Test cricket, because in the end the prospect of playing only county cricket proved too much for him and he gave it up.

I saw a video of Graeme Pollock batting against the 'rebel' West Indians, and he seemed to be in some trouble against the fast, short-pitched bowling which they served up. He had particular problems with Sylvester Clarke's bowling, though he is not unique in that. But everyone tells me that Pollock was a great player, and on his day he must have been a rare sight. He certainly enjoyed batting against the 'rebel' Australians, and they had lots of pace bowlers – Hogg, Alderman, McCurdy, Rackemann and Maguire.

Martin Crowe is currently New Zealand's top batsman, and he looks as if he will break all their records in due course. I have never bowled at him, but he seems to be a well-organised, compact player with a good defence and hungry for runs. It will be interesting to see how he copes in Test cricket after

Hadlee goes, because the rest of the team – with the possible exception of John Wright – is not of a particularly high standard, and Crowe will be under immense pressure to make runs all the time.

I am not a great judge of wicket-keepers, and I often find it difficult to assess their respective merits. However, I do know that there were three great keepers in my time. The first was Alan Knott, who was my wicket-keeper in Kerry Packer's World XI. I was amazed by the timing of Knott's takes: the ball would hit his gloves and you could hardly hear a sound. And his mobility was invaluable – he took catches down the leg side which some keepers would not have reached. He worked very hard and was a very humble man. I had the greatest respect for him.

I was also always impressed by Rodney Marsh of Australia. He may not have been as talented as Knott, but once again his mobility was amazing – the way he threw himself about when keeping to Lillee, Thomson and the other Australian pace bowlers was quite incredible.

Pakistan's Wasim Bari was another outstanding wicket-keeper, and certainly the best we have ever produced. He was not quite as mobile as Knott and Marsh – in fact if anything he was a little slow on the leg side. But he was brilliant on the off side, and his timing was excellent, so that once again barely a sound could be heard as the ball went into the gloves. He served Pakistan cricket well for many years, and we have not had a keeper of his calibre since his retirement. A good wicket-keeper makes a lot of difference, especially to the faster bowlers. I was very sorry when Wasim Bari retired, still more so since there was hardly a mention of his going in the press. He had played 81 Tests for Pakistan, making 228 dismissals, which put him third, behind Marsh and Knott, on the Test list, yet the media let him disappear without a sound.

CHAPTER 10

Captaincy

The captain whose example I always tried to follow was Ian Chappell. He had led the Australians in England in 1972, while I was still at school, and I remember that all of us at Worcester RGS were captivated by his aggressive style of leadership. He was dynamic and forceful, and above all he had the complete respect of his young team – something which became apparent when his inexperienced side fought Illingworth's vastly experienced England team all the way and drew the series 2-2. This was basically the side which, two years later, thrashed England in Australia to regain the Ashes. The series made a double impression on me, through the captaincy of Ian Chappell and the fast bowling of Dennis Lillee.

Five years later, I saw Ian Chappell captain the World Series Cricket Australian XI, and opposing him during those two seasons of Packer cricket made me appreciate what a great captain he was. The Australian team was not quite what it had been, and some of their players were being sorted out by the consistent fast bowling. They were certainly outgunned by the emerging West Indies side, with their battery of fast bowlers, while the World XI – of which I was a part – had great depth and all-round strength. Although probably the weakest of the three teams, the Australians consistently did well, and this was almost entirely due to the bowling of Dennis Lillee and the captaincy of Ian Chappell, who led by example, and expected his team to fight along with him. I've heard a lot about captains being good tacticians or having great strategical sense, but I am convinced that unless a captain can lead from the front, he cannot inspire his team to fight.

My captaincy was helped by my general approach to cricket. I've always been ambitious, and although I had not sought the captaincy, as soon as I had been appointed I quickly realised that I had gained another ambition – to lead Pakistan into becoming the best team in the world.

An advantage of aiming high is that one is never satisfied with one's performance. Hardly ever – especially in my early years in cricket – was I totally satisfied at the end of a match or a season. This unfulfilled feeling always made me strive for improvement. The hardest thing was to impart my ambitious approach to the Pakistan team, and to break through the negative attitudes that had prevailed for so long. In many ways we had brought these negative feelings upon ourselves, with our doctored, dead pitches which were prepared in such a way that the team were very unlikely to lose at home. The result was a team incapable of doing well under pressure, because the players were not used to it. Even when we were in with a chance of winning there was a tendency to panic, simply because the pressure was too great. Many times, outside Pakistan, we managed to lose matches from winning positions. A good example of this was Intikhab's tour of Australia in 1972–3. After being outplayed in the first Test, Pakistan scored 574 for 8 in the second – and lost! This was bad enough, but in the final Test Pakistan reduced Australia to 101 for 8 in their second innings, an overall lead of just 75, but the pressure got to them and two tail-enders took the score to 184. Even then Pakistan needed only 159 to win, but were bowled out by Lillee – who had a bad back – and the inexperienced Max Walker for 106. Australia won the series 3-0, although they should have lost it 2-1.

Because of this negative attitude, Pakistan's players were more concerned about personal failure than the team's success. No one embodied this more than Zaheer. His attitude to any match was that *he* must not fail: the bigger the crowd and the higher the expectations, the more worried he became. By contrast, my attitude has always been that the bigger the occasion and the crowd, the better I would play: I wanted to do well rather than worry about failure. Maybe I was lucky in coming from a relatively privileged background, in that I was never worried about cricket being my only means of support. Whatever the reason, I was never unduly concerned about losing or – above all – about possibly losing the captaincy. All I wanted was to do my best and ensure that the team fought as a unit against England in 1982. I thought it would be my last tour of England: I didn't think that I would still be around in 1987. Furthermore, England were lacking some of their better players, like Gooch, Emburey and Underwood, who had been banned after going on an unofficial tour of South Africa, so I thought that 1982 would provide us with our best-ever chance of defeating England.

I had toured England previously in 1971 and 1974. In 1971 we had lost the Leeds Test and the series after being in a winning position, while in 1974 we had the better side but all three matches were drawn. Like the other Packer players, I had to look on in 1978, when a second-rate Pakistan team was destroyed by an England team for whom Botham was performing miracles. The year 1982 seemed likely to provide my best, and last, chance of winning a series on English soil.

I soon recognised that the most important part of captaincy was team selection – rather like a Prime Minister choosing a Cabinet. I insisted on having control over team selection, because I couldn't see how I could plan an overall strategy without what I considered to be the best team. I remember that Javed Miandad wanted a certain player included in the side during the 1980–1 series against the West Indies, but the selectors refused. Later in that series I asked him why another player wasn't in the side, and Javed replied that once again he had wanted that particular player but the selectors had refused. I then spoke to the selectors, who came up with a different story altogether and claimed that Javed had wanted another player entirely. Neither the players nor the public knew who was really selecting the team. I made up my mind that I would insist on complete control over team selection. I realised that this made me responsible for the success or failure of the team: I could not – and would not – blame the selectors if we were unsuccessful.

When the team for England was being chosen, I felt that Abdul Qadir was the one bowler who was absolutely vital to my plans. Initially his selection was vetoed on the grounds that he would be unsuitable, in that the English pitches were unlikely to be helpful to spinners. I virtually had to say that if he wasn't included, I wouldn't go either, and in the end I was lucky to get the team that I wanted.

Since I wasn't unduly worried about losing the captaincy, I could gamble on the team selection: the risks were such that I backed my own judgement. If I felt a player was good enough, I backed him unreservedly. I wanted players to believe that the team was selected purely on merit, and not because a player was thought to be the captain's favourite or something like that, as had happened so often in the past. Many players could never be sure of a place simply because someone didn't like them. Once a player feels that he has been unjustly dropped, there is a great temptation for him to play for himself if he is recalled, even though he is usually a team man. This kind of thing doesn't happen if the players have faith in the captain, nor do I think that, during my time as captain, anyone has felt that he had been dropped from the team because I didn't like him personally, or because I was from Lahore and he was from Karachi, or some other fanciful reason.

I was never very keen on players who could be brilliant when there was no pressure, but folded up as soon as we were in trouble. This has always been a problem for Pakistani teams. After the England series I realised that we had a couple of players like that, so I kept a lookout for players on whom I could depend when the chips were down.

One such player is the wicket-keeper Salim Yousuf. He is not a natural wicket-keeper – something which soon becomes obvious when you study his technique closely – but when under pressure behind the stumps or with the bat he raises his game to unlikely levels. As far as I was concerned he would always be in my team, even if he had the odd bad match, because I knew he would usually take the important catch, or score a few runs at a crucial moment.

As captain I always tried to treat each player as an individual. I think this is important: too many captains have failed to realise that everyone is different, and needs to be treated differently. Everyone has his own personality and individuality – it's wrong to lump all the players together and treat the team like a flock of sheep. There are always some players who need to be encouraged, some who need to be pushed, and some who need to be treated in a particular way depending on their own eccentricities. A prime example of a player in this last category was Sarfraz Nawaz, for whose inclusion in the side during India's 1982–3 tour I had to fight tooth and nail. The Board wanted to follow a youth policy, and to include a younger player instead of Sarfraz, who by then was almost thirty-four. I've always believed that cricket is one sport in which experience counts above almost anything else, and I would only opt for a youngster if his ability exceeded that of an older player, or if he obviously had the potential to far outstrip the older man. Too often in Pakistan cricket a youngster has been included in the side in place of a more experienced player; the youngster fails and is dropped, often never to return. An example of this was Agha Zahid, who replaced Sadiq in the first Test against the West Indies in 1974–5. Zahid scored 14 and 1 and was dropped, and never played for Pakistan again. There were many other examples of players being taken on a tour who were never heard of again – Talaat Mirza, who went to India in 1979–80, is one who springs to mind.

As far as Sarfraz and the 1982–3 Indian series were concerned, I thought he would be a much better bet against the experienced Indian batting line-up than some untried colt. I met a lot of opposition from the selection committee, who in the end refused to accept his inclusion: it went all the way to the Board president, who finally agreed with me, so Sarfraz played against the Indians. He proved to be outstanding in the series, taking 19 wickets and bowling long spells. Of the young pace bowlers we tried, Jalaluddin took 2 for 152 and Tahir Naqqash 2 for 211. Yet Sarfraz had been omitted from our 1979–80 tour of India because Asif Iqbal, our then captain, felt that he couldn't handle him. On this subject I differ from Asif, in that I think it is the captain's duty to get along with his players, however awkward they might appear at times, and to handle them in the way that is most beneficial to the team as a whole.

A not dissimilar situation arose in New Zealand in 1984–5, when Javed Miandad sent Abdul Qadir home for 'disciplinary reasons'. This was extremely bad thinking on Javed's part: he should have realised that although Qadir wasn't doing well on the tour – and I think that was the real reason he was sent home – he was still an important member of the team. Had he been getting wickets I am sure that there is no way that he would have been sent home – other players have done much worse things on tour, but got away with it because their performances were good.

I think Javed should have made his peace with Qadir and kept him on the tour, bearing his future value to the team in mind, even though he was out of form. He should have tried to get the best out of him, rather than humiliating him on a flimsy 'disciplinary' excuse. In the end Javed and the Pakistan team suffered: New Zealand won the third Test at Dunedin, so taking the series, largely because Qadir was not playing. New Zealand needed 50 to win when Jeremy Coney was joined by Ewen Chatfield in what was, in effect, a last-wicket partnership, since Lance Cairns had been injured, and together they scored the necessary runs. Coney, who made 111 not out, was a great pressure player, but I find it hard to believe that Qadir would not have dismissed Chatfield, who was one of the worst batsmen in international cricket. As it was, Chatfield made 21 not out – his highest Test score – and New Zealand crept home.

Later that winter we played the World Championship of Cricket in Australia, and all our matches were on the Melbourne Cricket Ground at a time when the pitch was a spinners' paradise. The Indian leg-spinner Laxman Shivara-makrishnan – who was not in Qadir's league as a leg-spinner, and has subsequently disappeared from the international scene – proved to be one of the most successful bowlers of the championship, whereas Pakistan were without a leg-spinner. As a result, we lost to India in the final. Later on we went to Sharjah, and on the spinners' wicket there we bowled India out for 125. Although I took 6 for 14 we certainly missed Qadir. India then bowled us out for 87, a terrible score. Even as a batsman Qadir would have helped, for he is a good player of spin bowling, and of course he would have bowled well on that strip. With him in the team, I doubt if India would have reached 100.

Pakistan cricket suffered from Javed's hasty action in sending Qadir home. I would only send a player home if I realised that the team was suffering as a result of his character or his indiscipline. I would only take such a decision as a last resort.

I think Qadir seemed to perform better under my captaincy because I understood his temperament. I always knew that he needed a lot of encouragement, in that he loses confidence very quickly; and that he had to be taken off if he was hit about, because once his confidence has been shattered it takes a long time to return. He started badly on the 1986–7 tour of India, and his confidence gradually ebbed away. Rather than criticise, I encouraged him, often taking him off to save him being hammered. I even dropped him from the Test team because the pitch looked too good and I didn't think he could take a beating at the hands of the Indian batsmen. I was not only thinking in terms of the Indian series, but of the forthcoming England tour as well, and even the World Cup. A captain must look ahead, and he must act in the long-term interests of the team wherever possible.

I'm always annoyed when players play for themselves and not for the team, and when I saw this happening I made my displeasure known in no uncertain terms. During the 1983–4 tour of Australia one of the batsmen got to about 30, at which point he realised that the second new ball was nearly due. So he hit out at everything, trying to get a few runs before the new ball was taken. In some circumstances this tactic is justified, but not on this occasion. I made sure that not only the player concerned, but the whole squad, realised my displeasure and understood that this should not happen again. It is important that a captain should make his feelings known to the team – it's fatal to keep your thoughts to yourself. Players must realise that slackness like this will not be tolerated, and that there cannot be any team spirit if players play simply for themselves and their own averages. I played in too many Pakistan teams where batsmen made useful forties or fifties and then walked out, looking very pleased with themselves, even though the team went on to lose the match. I tried to make players realise that these flashy fifties are not what win Tests: what is wanted is a grafting innings. Even if a player has 150 to his name he should not feel that he has done enough.

It has given me great pleasure to watch the present Pakistan team develop into a cohesive, fighting unit. The hallmark of a fighting team with fierce team spirit is the attitude of the tail-enders: when the later batsmen hang around at the crease it shows the whole team that the fight is on in earnest. It also makes it clear which tail-enders have got the right attitude. Since the match against the West Indies at Faisalabad in 1986–7, the Pakistan team has always fought down the order to the last man. Even the match at Bangalore against India in 1986–7 was effectively won by the tail-end batsmen – indeed, on that whole Indian tour our tail always wagged to great effect.

Whenever there was a crisis during the 1987 World Cup, our tail seemed to come to the rescue. I'll never forget the group match against the West Indies, when Abdul Qadir, helped by Salim Jaffer, scored 14 off Courtney Walsh's last over of the match to win. Earlier, what seemed a hopeless position had been retrieved by Salim Yousuf, who scored 56. That is what team spirit means: the whole side is trying to win, nor do the bowlers leave all the batting to the recognised batsmen. The current Pakistan team's greatest asset is that they won't give up. Ironically, I felt a sense of fulfilment when we lost the World Cup semi-final to Australia. We were always up against it, but at no time did the team ever contemplate defeat. Even when we needed 18 to win and our last batsman, Tauseef Ahmed, had to bat with virtually one hand – he had two stitches in his other hand, which he had injured while attempting a return catch – the other players were sure that we would pull off another unlikely victory. When Tauseef was out a sense of shock ran through the dressing-room, as though the players could not believe that they had lost.

This previously unknown team spirit in the Pakistani dressing-room resulted in our winning Tests against India and England when conditions favoured our more experienced opponents. I have played in Pakistan teams with more talent and experience than the present one, but half the players were what are known in county cricket as 'Jack-men', as in 'I'm all right, Jack'.

Occasionally I was criticised for certain tactical moves, but it is often easy to be wise after the event. If you fail, there will always be critics, whereas if you are successful – even if you have sometimes made tactical errors – everyone will forget and praise you.

Of course I believe that a captain should have tactical sense, and in this respect I was probably lucky to have played so much county cricket, where one cannot help but pick up the finer points of strategy by playing day in and day out. You also, almost automatically, pick up the weaknesses of the other players.

The most important aspect of captaincy is when your side is in the field. There is not much you can do to influence your batsmen – you can tell them what conditions are like and what are the strengths of the other side's bowlers, but basically they are on their own. If you are a reasonable batsman, you can lead by example, playing sensibly and hoping that the others will follow suit. But in the field everything is down to the captain. Where possible, the right bowlers have to be brought on to face particular batsmen; conditions have to be assessed; field-placings have to be altered.

Although the bowler-captain has to think about all this *and* his own bowling, I think that being a bowler helped my captaincy a great deal. Having bowled in different conditions, I felt confident of handling my attack, and capable of advising the younger bowlers in the side. It was easy for me to advise and encourage them, because I understood what they were trying to do. I could go up to a bowler and say, 'The wind is blowing from over there, so the ball will probably swing in this direction,' or tell them that they were bowling too short or too full or too erratically. When I was younger, I always resented a batsman telling me how to bowl: it is much easier to accept criticism from a fellow bowler. The standard captain's remark – 'Just bowl a line and length' – is useless: every fool knows that you *should* be bowling a line and length, but what matters is why you are *not* doing so. I used to study a bowler's run-up and delivery, and suggest what he might be doing wrong, or slight alterations which might improve his bowling.

If a bowler delivered a long-hop, my comment – if any – was not the standard parrot-cry of 'Pitch it up'. I'd ask if everything was all right, and whether he was having trouble with his run-up, his action or his rhythm. Often something quite small can throw a bowler off – for example, he may be running uphill without realising it – with the result that his direction or length goes. Under these circumstances the last thing a bowler wants is his captain bawling at him.

Sometimes the batsman-captain fails to understand what is happening with the ball. I mentioned earlier how, in Barbados in 1976–7, Mushtaq insisted on taking the new ball even though Sarfraz and I both wanted to continue with the old one. We were right, and the new ball got thrashed about all over the park. There should always be a good reason for taking a new ball, and it should never be taken simply because it has fallen due.

Allan Border tells me that he did not fully understand what his pace bowlers were trying to do, and is honest enough to admit that he did not know what advice to offer them when they were being hit: he wishes he had had an experienced bowler in the side – someone like Lillee – to help them out. My own problem was understanding the particular problems faced by spinners. I was probably not much good at advising them, though over the years I tried to understand them more, and to help them without knowing the finer points of spin bowling.

During its brief Test history, Pakistan has probably had more captains than other countries over the same period. One reason for this was that the loss of a series often meant the loss of the captaincy, so the captain was always under pressure. This frequent jettisoning of skippers led to younger, inexperienced players having the captaincy thrust upon them before they were ready for it. My cousin Javed Burki, for example, was appointed captain for the 1962 England tour, when he was only twenty-four. Although too young then, he would have made a good captain later in the 1960s – but he was never tried again after the disasters in England, when Pakistan lost 4-0. I was always impressed by his captaincy of Lahore during my first few seasons in first-class cricket.

Pakistan's first, and probably best, captain was Abdul Hafeez Kardar. He had authority and the respect of the team, and he was a fighter. He led the Pakistan side in England in 1954 which won the Oval Test and drew the series.

Mushtaq Mohammad captained the side for some time and did pretty well, at least to begin with. He started off as a very good captain, but later, as his confidence against the faster bowlers faded, he became more and more negative. He had the confidence of the players; he stuck up for them; he had earned the respect of the team by being a senior member of a good side. Unfortunately, by the end of his tenure as captain he was ultra-defensive. I'll never forget the Perth Test of 1978–9, when we were playing an Australian side which, in the absence of their Packer players, was really only a second eleven. Before the match Mushtaq decided that we would play for a draw, but having started out in such a negative frame of mind we managed to lose. So, too, I felt that the team would have made a better fist of saving the match at Kingston, Jamaica in 1976–7 had Mushtaq led from the front. But he let the team see that he was worried about his own safety in the face of some hostile fast bowling; the fight went out of the team, and we lost the match in a quite pathetic fashion, with only a brave century from Asif Iqbal and a flashy 64 from Wasim Raja saving our faces to some extent.

Asif Iqbal took over from Mushtaq for the 1979 World Cup and the following winter's tour of India. Our team was better than the results suggested, and he was very unlucky with injuries. In Pakistan eyes, however, he had committed the cardinal sin of losing to India, and he knew he had to go. He resigned before the team arrived home, but would probably have been sacked anyway.

It was unfair on Javed Miandad, Asif's successor, to have been made captain at such a young age. He too had to contend with a number of senior players within the team who were slighted by his appointment, and unfortunately he was not mature enough then to handle them properly. Instead of appeasing them he antagonised them: this contributed to the players' revolt of 1981–2, when a number of senior players said they would not tour England under Javed's captaincy. What surprised me about the revolt was that Javed allowed it to happen: he should have realised that he was out of his depth and resigned, instead of trying to continue with another team.

The other captain of my time, of course, was Zaheer Abbas. Zaheer's case reminds me of the tragedy of Macbeth: no one had ever wanted the captaincy as much or as openly as Zaheer, but in the end he found the burden so great that he had to give it up. For some reason, which I don't understand, he had always wanted to captain Pakistan. He conspired against the reigning captains, trying to pull them down and take their place. In the end he took into the team a player whom he knew to be not good enough, but who, he felt, had to be in the side to support him in the captaincy; and by now he had lost the respect of the rest of the team. As captain, he was entirely defensive, because he couldn't afford to lose – as we have seen, losing a series often means the end of the Pakistan captain's reign. Under Zaheer, Pakistan managed to draw a Test with India which it would have been easier to win – he just couldn't face the possibility of losing.

All in all, I think that his priorities were wrong: he wanted to be captain more than to be a leader, and the perks of captaincy more than the responsibility of the job. In the end it got too much for him. New Zealand came to play in Pakistan: Pakistan won 2–0, and there were a lot of umpiring controversies. At one point New Zealand, who were without Richard Hadlee, almost walked off the field in protest at a decision from Shakoor Rana – a name that was to become more familiar during England's troubled tour of 1987–8. Jeremy Coney, the Kiwis' captain, said that Pakistan had cheated in order to win the series. That same winter Pakistan were to go to New Zealand and face their full side, including Hadlee. Although he had been appointed for a full year, Zaheer refused to captain the side in New Zealand on the grounds of being mentally exhausted, and gave up the captaincy which had meant so much to him. Under Javed once again, Pakistan lost the series 2–0, with Hadlee taking 16 wickets – but, as we have seen, they might have got away with a 1-1 draw if Abdul Qadir had not been sent home before the final Test.

As far as other countries' captains are concerned, the only Indian skipper who impressed me was Sunil Gavaskar, mainly because of his extensive knowledge of the game. People talk about Mike Brearley as the outstanding cricket brain, but I think that Gavaskar lost nothing by comparison. He was a very sound captain, and had to cope with the knowledge that often his only hope was to draw matches, because India's bowling attack was not good enough to bowl out the other side twice. It may be that this sense of frustration eventually led him to give up the captaincy. He captained India against me in the 1982–3 series which we won – although his leadership was good, our team was much better. Gavaskar produced one of the best spells of captaincy I have seen when he led India to success in the World Championship of Cricket in Australia in 1984–5, and the way in which he handled his bowling resources was quite brilliant.

Gavaskar suffered far more abuse from the Indian press than he deserved. As we have seen, factions are polarised between the two major Indian cricketing centres of Bombay and Delhi, just as they are between Lahore and Karachi in Pakistan. Gavaskar came from Bombay, and no matter what he achieved, he could never win over the Delhi writers. In the end, he realised that India were unlikely to do well in Tests with the side he had, and I think he was frustrated by the public's apparent inability to distinguish between the tactics necessary for Tests and one-day matches. The Indian public did not seem to be able to understand that the two versions of the game are very different – they thought that if India was so successful in one-day cricket, they ought to win Test matches as well. In the end, I believe, Sunil got fed up with the extra pressure.

I thought that Tony Greig had the most charisma among English captains. Surprisingly, though, his captaincy seemed to undergo the same sort of transformation as Mushtaq's, in that it became more defensive when he lost form and confidence. He relied on leadership from the front, so when his playing contribution declined his captaincy form went as well.

Another English captain I rated highly was Keith Fletcher, whom I always found a shrewd tactician in county cricket. I never played against him in Tests when he was captain – he only led England in one rather unsatisfactory series in India – but I think he was harshly treated by the TCCB.

Mike Brearley is considered one of the all-time great captains, and there is no doubt that he had a good cricket brain and was tactically sound. But I can't rate him an outstanding captain, because I don't think he was a good enough player to merit a Test place. A lot is made of Brearley's tactical genius, but a closer look at his successes shows that most of them took place during the Packer era. Brearley won 5-1 in Australia against a depleted and inexperienced team; he also beat an average New Zeland team, and a mediocre Pakistan side in 1978 which was lacking our Packer players. He never captained against the West Indies, and when he took on the full Australian side in 1979–80, Greg Chappell's team won 3-0.

He will probably be best remembered for the Australian rubber in 1981. After Botham had been removed as captain, Brearley took over again, and but for an incredible performance by Botham and Willis at Headingley, he would have started off with a thumping defeat. Botham – who seemed to sparkle once he had been relieved of the captaincy – did it again at Edgbaston and at Old Trafford, and England ran out easy winners in the series: Brearley was hailed as the conquering hero, and was given much of the credit for Botham's magical performances. Yet if Brearley was as great as he was cracked up to be, he should have done better than the 3-0 defeat in 1979–80, inflicted by an Australian team which was probably past its prime and was comprehensively beaten by the West Indians that same summer.

Captaining a team is not that difficult if you're playing against weak opposition. The problems start when you're playing a better team and are struggling. That is when the captain's job becomes most important, and when he must lead from the front. I don't think Brearley was capable of doing that.

I thought David Gower did as good a job as he could during those series when England was being rolled over by the West Indies. He tried to lead them from the front – he scored more runs than anyone else in West Indies in 1985–6 – but the rest of the team were unable to follow him. He had done marvellously well against India and Australia, but the selectors were almost obliged to change a captain who had lost successive series to the West Indies by five matches to nil.

As I've said before, the greatest captain of my time was undoubtedly Ian Chappell. He had all the right qualities: he played a number of important innings when Australia were up against it, and he led from the front. His fighting captaincy during the Packer years was a revelation to me. I was playing for the World XI in Perth early in 1978, and we ran up a huge total of 625, with Barry Richards scoring 207, Viv Richards 177 and Gordon Greenidge 140. When the Australians came in to bat, Roberts and I took a few wickets and they were soon struggling to avoid the follow-on. Ian Chappell was batting, and he took a nasty blow on the top hand from Roberts's bouncer. Everyone could tell it was a bad injury: his hand was obviously broken because he could hardly hold the bat with it. But he kept on batting with only one hand, facing Roberts and hooking Tony Greig for four, and provided an inspiration to the rest of his team.

Ian Chappell had a good many problems with the Australian Cricket Board, because his appointment as captain coincided with the commercial explosion within the game. World cricket was becoming more professional, and the Board was trying to resist this trend. Chappell fought for his players, and in doing so made himself a few enemies in high places. His association with Kerry Packer, of course, did nothing to endear him to the traditional rulers of the game. The so-called 'Chappell era' was a very important period in world cricket: the players were beginning to discover their true worth, and Ian Chappell was in the vanguard. Some ugly aspects of the game become more apparent during his time as captain, including the distasteful 'sledging' of batsmen by the close fielders, which I have always found achieves nothing except to promote bad blood between the teams. On the whole, you don't get good players out by sledging: I prefer the West Indian approach, whereby a meaningful look or glare says everything, without having to resort to verbal abuse.

Greg Chappell followed his brother, and he too was a good captain. He was tactically sound, had the respect of his players and was a doughty fighter. Had he come first, he might be remembered as a great captain, but as it is he was over-shadowed by his brother.

After Greg's tenure as captain, Australian cricket went into decline. Kim Hughes, who followed the Chappells, was another of those captains who was more loyal to his office than to his team, which is why he never had the respect of his players, most of whom felt anyway that Rod Marsh was the obvious choice to follow Greg Chappell.

On the whole, Australian cricketers are the most patriotic I know. Their national character is such that they will generally fight hard no matter who the captain is, but somehow under Hughes this wasn't the case. I thought it tragic that Hughes eventually felt compelled to resign the captaincy at a press conference, during which he burst into tears – which showed how much the captaincy had meant to him. No doubt there is some similarity between his case and that of Zaheer Abbas.

Among West Indian captains, Clive Lloyd stands out, though it must be said that he was helped by having so many great players at the same time. He had the pick of some of the greatest fast bowlers of all time, plus the batting of Viv Richards, the greatest batsman of his day, and Gordon Greenidge, who wasn't that far behind. In some ways he was lucky to be in charge of one of the best teams in cricket history. His greatest feat was to bring them all together and make them play, turning them from a group of talented individuals into a great team. He himself became a respected father-figure to most of his players.

Lloyd was widely criticised by some sections of the English media for encouraging short-pitched bowling. This struck me as unfair: I don't think that they over-indulged in bouncers, since their fast bowlers were quite good enough to get people out without bothering about short-pitched bowling. Obviously there were times when the fast bowlers got excited and let a few bouncers go, but it is a natural reaction if you find you're bowling on a fast pitch or if you're being hit around. The captain has yet to be born who would tell a group of fast bowlers of the kind that Lloyd had at his disposal to ease up on the short-pitched stuff.

Lloyd was a great ambassador for the West Indies, and his was a hard act to follow. He did make a few tactical errors. In Australia in 1984–5, he was 3-0 up in the series and on top in the fourth Test at Melbourne. Surprisingly, he chose to bat on for a while on the final morning, and set Australia an imposs-ible target. Then, as most people expected, Australia collapsed against the fast bowlers, but they managed to hang on in the end, with eight wickets down. On the whole, though, he was a great captain for that particular team.

It was never going to be easy to follow Clive Lloyd, and Viv Richards drew the short straw. It is very unfair to compare Richards's performance with Lloyd's because Richards in-herited a team which was beginning to lose some of its great players. Lloyd, of course, had gone – and has yet to be adequately replaced – Roberts and Croft had retired, Holding, Garner and Gomes were near the end. Even so, Richards blitzed England 5-0 in the Caribbean. I think that Viv is going to be a great captain: he leads from the front, and he has the complete respect of his team. My only criticism of him is that he is too volatile and sometimes finds it hard to control his temper. One of the most crucial things I learned from captain-ing Pakistan and from watching other captains was that different kinds of teams need different kinds of captains.

1. Middlesex v. Sussex, 27 May 1986. We dismissed Middlesex for 70, during the course of which I produced my best-ever bowling in the County Championship – 8 for 34

2. General Zia meeting the team during the 1987 'cricket diplomacy' tour of India

3. Bangalore, 1987. The moment of victory – we had beaten India by 16 runs and won the series. Also in the picture are Wasim Akram (*right*) and Javed Miandad, who had picked up Iqbal Qasim

4. The press conference before the first Test against England, Old Trafford, 1987

5. My 300th Test wicket: Jack Richards caught by Ijaz Ahmed during the third Test against England at Headingley, 1987

6. Ian Botham bowls me a bouncer during the fourth Test against England at Edgbaston, 1987 . . .

7. . . . and I return the compliment

8. Wasim Akram is a young all-rounder of enormous talent – and immense enthusiasm. Here he celebrates dismissing Ian Botham, caught and bowled

9. The end of the series in England, 1987. I thought we should have won by at least two Tests

10. With the Man of the Series trophy

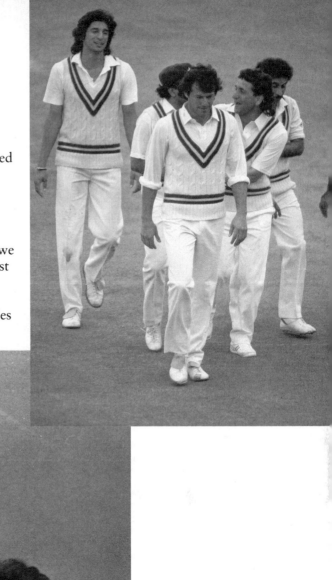

11. With Sunil Gavaskar during the MCC Bicentenary match at
Lord's in 1987

CHAPTER 11

County Cricket

English county cricket is, without any doubt, the most professionally organised structure of its kind in the world. England is the only country to have seventeen teams of such a high standard: other cricketing countries would be lucky to have half, or even a quarter, as many teams of such quality. More cricket is played in England in one season than is played in other countries in three or four.

There is no better school in which to learn how to play cricket and to polish one's talent. Batting is a most difficult art, and the best possible way to develop one's skills is through county cricket. During the season a batsman is exposed to all sorts of bowling on different wickets, each with its own particular characteristics. Since no cricket is being played anywhere else in the world during the English season, each county is in a position to include in its team top international pace attackers, such as Hadlee, Rice, Marshall, Holding and Le Roux. A player has a marvellous opportunity to study great batsmen in action. Certainly I developed as a player by watching top players and experimenting as a result.

Bowlers also learn a great deal by playing so frequently and on such differing wickets. To begin with, I simply enjoyed bowling fast. Later on I learned that although going flat out was productive at Hove – when it was fast in the Seventies – a different approach was needed on a deadly slow wicket, such as Headingley or Edgbaston. Again, one had to change one's approach altogether for one-day cricket; and within one-day matches, the line and length in the initial overs had to be different from those in the final overs. Medium-pacers tend to learn most from county cricket, in that conditions are ideal for them. After two seasons in county cricket, most bowlers understand how to exploit English conditions. Richard Hadlee, for example, improved enormously from playing county cricket, and became a master of bowling on wickets that favoured any seam.

County cricket also makes a cricketer very sound tactically. Experience is essential in cricket, since there are so many different situations and conditions which batsmen and bowlers have to face. Apart from playing against many different teams in many different conditions, one learns from the 'old pros'. The average age in county cricket is the highest in the world. Each team will have a few players in their thirties, and some even in their forties. In other countries if a player is unlikely to play Test cricket he will be dropped in favour of a youngster. Yet many county cricketers keep on playing well into their thirties, even if they have never played for England and have little chance of doing so; and one of the ways in which senior players can be extremely valuable is by imparting useful knowledge to young cricketers.

I learned a lot by talking and listening to the experienced Worcestershire cricketers, Gifford and D'Oliveira. When I arrived in Worcestershire as an eighteen-year-old, I hadn't a clue about the things every cricketer was assumed to know. I learned and developed much of my technique by listening to and watching such players, and was hardly ever coached. On occasions, when I got out, they told me when I was back in the dressing-room that they had seen it coming to me. They could often tell when and how a particular batsman would get out. In the same way, my bowling mistakes would be pointed out to me. In the final analysis, of course, it is up to the individual cricketer to decide when to follow advice and when to follow his instincts. In my early days at Worcester I was told that I should stick to medium-paced inswing bowling rather than the fast stuff.

Pakistan and the West Indies are the two countries to benefit most from county cricket. The Pakistani batting might of the Seventies was almost entirely due to team members playing for various counties who returned home and raised the standard of our domestic cricket – Mushtaq and Intikhab to begin with, and then Asif, Majid, Sadiq, Younis and Sarfraz. Zaheer and I followed during the Seventies, and Javed Miandad in 1976.

How is it that overseas players have gained so much from county cricket, while England has declined in cricketing power since the 1970s – or at least has failed to produce outstanding teams? There is no doubt that, such is the richness of English cricket, England could produce two or even three teams of Test standard at any one time; yet there have been few truly great English players over the last eighteen years or so. I believe that various factors are responsible for this, including the growth of one-day cricket.

At present there is one three-day competition and three one-day competitions. One-day cricket has been necessary for the financial security of county cricket by bringing back the crowds. Fielding, running between the wickets and improvisation in batting have been revolutionised by it, enriching the game in the process. However, the quality of play has suffered as a result of the sheer volume of one-day cricket. To begin with, it has more than doubled the amount of travelling involved. Playing cricket seven days a week begins to take its toll by mid-season. Still worse is the physical strain of one-day cricket, and it is this that makes present-day cricket so very different to what it was before the 1970s. A Sunday afternoon match of forty overs can take more out of one than two days of a three-day match. On the Monday of a championship match, one can often see players suffering a hangover from a Sunday League match.

Since there are three one-day competitions, some counties concentrate on these and actually neglect three-day cricket. Somerset succeeded in multiplying their membership by winning one-day competitions, even though their results in the three-day championship were not good.

Young bowlers have suffered most from the advent of

one-day cricket. Apart from the extra physical pressure caused by increased travelling and the strenuous nature of the game, the short Sunday League run-ups are a major cause of injuries. It takes much more out of a bowler if he is trying to bowl fast off a short run-up. I was extremely lucky that, between the age of eighteen and twenty-three, I was a medium-pacer. I don't think one's body is strong enough to take the full impact of fast bowling until one is about twenty-three. A young pace bowler needs careful grooming, since a serious injury at this stage can ruin a fast bowler's career. Dennis Lillee suffered a stress fracture of his back when he was twenty-two, and both Essex's Neil Foster and Tony Pigott of Sussex had to have pins inserted in their backs when they came into county cricket. I remember watching these two bowlers when they started: both were trying to impress their respective counties and were coming in flat out in every match. Their captains saw they had pace and were understandably reluctant to take them off when they were doing so well, without realising that, at their ages, they needed to be looked after. Eventually something went wrong.

I remember watching Chris Old in 1971 at Bradford. He was developing into a genuine fast bowler. On occasions in 1974 he bowled as fast as anyone. But although he possessed a fine bowling action, day-in, day-out cricket was too much for him, and after a series of injuries he settled down as a medium-pacer. Indeed, the current structure of county cricket encourages bowlers to become medium-pacers.

On the whole, overseas fast bowlers remain unaffected because, by the time they join counties, they are established players, their actions have stabilised, and they are physically mature enough to take the strain. Even so, not many fast bowlers can go flat out in county cricket for more than two seasons. Andy Roberts and Courtney Walsh both failed to sustain their pace in their third seasons, though Hadlee and Marshall are exceptions. Neither of the two outstanding English fast bowlers of my time, Snow and Willis, bowled much in county cricket. The fastest English bowler today,

Graham Dilley, has had a good many injuries, and has realised that the only way to keep himself fit is by pacing himself in county cricket.

The nature of county cricket is such as to rule out amateur players of the kind that flourish in other cricketing countries. Late developers have no chance of playing for England. Someone like Rick McCosker, who made his debut for Australia at the age of twenty-eight, might have missed out in England. If he wasn't prepared to play seven day a week cricket, he would have had no chance to represent his country.

I knew a couple of players at Oxford who had the talent but could not risk playing seven day a week cricket for two or three years only to discover that they were not good enough – especially as they had offers of jobs in the City. Compared to tennis, let alone soccer, county cricket is not that rewarding financially. A player who goes on to play for England can earn well, but how many young cricketers of twenty or twenty-two can be sure of playing Test cricket? Yet in Australia a youngster can hold down a job and still play Grade cricket. As soon as he is good enough he will be invited to play Sheffield Shield cricket, with a chance of playing for Australia.

The purpose of a three-day championship is to prepare players for Test cricket, but given the way it has evolved in England over the last fifteen years, I don't feel it is fulfilling its purpose. Unless the game is somehow contrived, it's impossible to get a result if two teams are evenly matched. Since the Seventies, the difference between the top and the bottom teams has been reduced by the arrival of overseas cricketers; and because of one-day competitions, and the strain of one-day matches, teams have tended not to force results in county matches. Especially after mid-season, two teams will often do little more than go through the motions on the first two days. On the last day the two captains will agree on a certain target to be chased by the team batting last, and this will depend on the wicket and the batting resources of whichever team bats first. Thereafter it becomes a one-day match. This is all very well if the purpose of the game is to produce a result and entertain a handful of spectators, but as a preparation for Test cricket, this type of cricket is not nearly competitive enough. I can hardly remember a Test match in which results have been contrived in this way. Teams have to be bowled out twice to win a Test match, which means that bowlers have to get batsmen out rather than rely on bowling line and length. Some counties end up under-preparing their wickets so as to fix a result – Nottinghamshire very successfully won the county championship twice in this way.

I have always believed that sixteen four-day matches would make the county championship a better preparation for Test cricket. The longer games would lay a greater emphasis on wicket-taking, so there should be more attacking bowlers in line for Test places. Middle-order batsmen would have a chance to build an innings, and the spinners could well play a bigger part on the last day. More days off would be an enormous relief to over-worked fast bowlers.

As I said earlier, one of the great – and unique – features of English cricket is the 'old pro', and every county has two or three such characters. For them, cricket is a job, and they have played for so long that they are basically fairly bored by it all. Most of them go through the seasons complaining it's too hot, or too cold, or too wet, or that the wicket is too slow, or too fast, and never in their favour, and so on and so forth. Anything new is deeply disliked – one-day cricket, for example, or team stretching exercises before the match, or overseas cricketers. Coloured overseas cricketers are particularly disliked since the 'old pros' are usually slightly racist. According to one of them one should 'never trust a black man': most of them are quite open about their racist views, unless of course the overseas player happens to be a nasty fast bowler. Their understanding of the game is excellent, which is the main reason for their surviving in county cricket for so long. They know and play within their limitations, which means that they are at their best under pressure. I have found them to be extremely self-effacing if they do well, whereas cricketers in Pakistan are completely the opposite, bragging about how they scored a brilliant 20, while the 'old pro' would be embarrassed if he scored a century.

Because of his understanding of the game he spots talent very quickly, but is then envious, rather like the old man Salieri is of Mozart in *Amadeus*. They always told me not to experiment with my bowling action lest I lose whatever I had. A draw is a good result for them. Arnold Long, the ex-captain of Sussex, who came from this school, preferred Wessels, a defensive player, to Javed Miandad, who is a match winner.

The 'old pro' is pro-establishment because his priority is keeping the job which provides him with his bread and butter. He hates controversies of any kind, especially with an umpire. I was once bowling to Trevor Jesty of Hampshire when Arnold Long was the Sussex captain and wicket-keeper. Jesty went back to a ball that came back and kept low, hitting his pads plumb in front. We all appealed, but to my amazement the umpire gave 'not out'. Utterly disbelieving, I asked him why he hadn't given Jesty out, and he said that the ball had hit him outside the line of the off stump. I went over to Long and asked what had happened. He shook his head and said 'Not out – it was missing the leg stump!' The 'old pro' is usually quite honest. For instance if he is caught behind and gets away with it, he admits it afterwards in the dressing-room. When Norman Gifford arrived back from an Indian tour in the mid-Seventies, he admitted that, through the English team's gamesmanship, they had managed to intimidate the Indian umpires into giving Gavaskar out caught bat and pad on quite a few occasions when he wasn't out.

I enjoyed the way in which these cricketers considered themselves superior to footballers, insisting on wearing a jacket and tie and carrying a briefcase when they arrived at the ground. Their kit was always immaculate, and I was often ticked off for looking too scruffy. They tended to enjoy horse racing, and the suspension of play due to rain. Without any doubt the best hours of the day for them were spent in the pub after the day's play. During home matches they could only spend a couple of hours in the pub, but on away matches, the entire evening might be spent there – after the customary 'clocking in' phone call to the wife, of course.

Whenever England have had a bad series in the past fifteen years, some papers have inevitably blamed overseas cricketers for the decline of English cricket. They argue that key positions in county teams are taken up by foreigners, and that this retards the development of local talent. At a Cricketers' Association meeting in 1977, 60 per cent of the members voted that English cricket would benefit if it was rid of overseas cricketers. I find this view totally illogical. Erecting trade barriers to protect the home industry must be counter-productive: sport is a field in which greater competition raises standards. South Africa has suffered so much through isolation that a rebel West Indian team – which was not even the equivalent of a West Indian second eleven – went to South Africa and thrashed their national team.

I wish that in Pakistan we could have two world-class cricketers per first-class team. I am sure we would become unbeatable. We have so much talent, but our domestic cricket is of such a poor standard that it is impossible to polish it here in Pakistan. The young county cricketer has such an excellent opportunity to play with and against great players.

Of course in the early Seventies the regulations allowed the counties to take on too many overseas players, and that was potentially harmful. At one stage Warwickshire had five in the team. But two per county is reasonable, and if top players were not being produced within the county system, then there had to be other serious structural deficiencies. It was their own fault if youngsters could not learn from Rice and Hadlee and others of that calibre. The two English players who are kept out by overseas cricketers will probably be marginal players anyway, with no chance of ever representing England. If it is true that overseas players are keeping English players out in the counties, then Yorkshire should have supplied the bulk of the English Test team. Yorkshire were always one of the strongest counties and have arrogantly refused to be contaminated by foreign players: yet after the arrival of overseas cricketers, they were no longer the power they had been in county cricket, nor have they supplied many players to the English Test team.

CHAPTER 12

Pakistan Cricket

The history of Pakistani cricket is one of nepotism, inefficiency, corruption and constant bickering. It is also the story of players who have risen above the mire. A cricketer needs immense talent, belief in himself and sheer luck to survive the political maze of our cricket. There have been brief periods when the BCCP has tried to promote cricket, but by and large its function has been to assert mindless authority and blunder through. The well-being of the players has usually been last on its list of priorities. Our Players' Association was actually wrecked by the BCCP in 1981 by their using the Sharjah benefit scheme. Our present first-class structure is a fair indication of the BCCP's inability to understand the game.

Pakistan's first Test cricketers were the product of a competitive first-class cricket system – the Pentangular structure that existed in pre-Partition India. Though underpaid, underfit and inexperienced, they possessed fighting qualities that enabled them to make the best use of their talents.

A. H. Kardar, our first captain, had played Test cricket for India before Partition. He was an astute cricketer who stressed discipline, teamwork and grit. Under his stewardship Pakistan performed creditably and even drew a series against a powerful English side in 1954, beating them at The Oval. Kardar retired in 1958 and Pakistani cricket was thrown to the wolves, the cricket bureaucrats whose progeny still rule the game. For a decade and a half, the Pakistani team sank into oblivion. A series of draws on placid pitches at home and resounding defeats abroad were capped by the loss of a home series to New Zealand in 1969–70. In twenty years Pakistan had produced only one world-class cricketer who was entirely the product of domestic cricket – Hanif Mohammad. The seeds of all the ills that plague our cricket were sown in this period.

The 1971 tour of England marked the beginning of a renaissance. The 1971 squad contained a number of gifted young players who surprised themselves, and the British public, by their performances. At that time English counties were on the lookout for overseas players, some of whom were already playing county cricket. The rest were quickly snapped up, and soon almost the entire Test team was playing first-class cricket in England as Zaheer, Asif, Mushtaq, Sadiq, Intikhab, Sarfraz, Majid, myself and, later, Javed Miandad joined the county scene. I am convinced that the sustained quality of our cricket in the 1970s – and to some extent even today – was primarily a result of the experience we gained playing in England. The daily grind and professionalism of county cricket honed our talent. By the mid-1970s we were able to take on the powerful Australian and West Indian teams on equal terms. Majid's rapid decline after he stopped playing for Glamorgan is proof of our debt to county cricket. That team contained only one player of genuine class who was a purely domestic product – Wasim Bari, the wicket-keeper.

The BCCP chose not to recognise that the dramatic resurgence of Pakistan's cricket had nothing to do with our own first-class structure. It was convenient to bask in the glory and take the credit while the going was good. A long-term strategy required hard work and serious thought. With the turnstiles humming, some of the BCCP bureaucrats were too busy building their own little empires to bother much about a future which had already been mortgaged.

It had been Kardar's idea to hand over our first-class cricket to banks, airlines, railways and other commercial institutions. Players were given jobs by Habib Bank, Pakistan International Airlines and the like. This was supposed to secure their financial futures. It soon became obvious that the public couldn't care a damn whether United Bank beat Pakistan Railways in the final of the Quaid-i-Azam Trophy, our premier domestic competition. First-class matches in which half a dozen Test players might be involved never attracted more than about a hundred spectators. Even so, for the companies that now controlled the game, cricket provided cheap and effective institutional advertising through newspaper and television coverage.

The companies had all the advantages and none of the responsibilities. They were supposed to own or maintain grounds, but it was easier to hire grounds for matches instead. Sometimes teams arrived at the ground to find that the pitch had not been prepared or that the match had been shifted to another venue. Because the pitches were under-prepared, fast bowlers were generally under-employed. I have taken part in matches in which the opening bowlers were spinners. The groundsmen were accountable to no one, and did not have to submit reports on the state of the pitch. The wickets at the major Test centres, particularly Karachi and Lahore, were destroyed through overuse. At one of the first-class grounds, sixteen matches were played on two strips with one-day intervals. General Safdar Butt, president of the BCCP, who was also chairman of WAPDA (the Water and Power Development Authority) told me when he took over that he could produce three types of pitch – fast, faster and fastest – through the expertise of WAPDA soil experts. Vast sums of money were spent in transporting Nandipur mud from an area near Sialkot. One or two pitches were actually destroyed in the process. On a supposedly 'fastest' wicket at the Gaddafi Stadium, Lahore, our pace bowlers were thrashed by the Sri Lankans for 228 runs in 38 overs in a one-day international. The pitch was slow and had an even lower bounce than usual. I confronted the General, but before he could reply Colonel Rafi Naseem, the BCCP secretary, intervened, eager to justify this huge expense, and claimed that I was making much ado about nothing – after all, Pakistan *had* taken seven Sri Lankan wickets in the process.

The present system provides a thoroughly inadequate grounding for Test cricket. The lack of public interest has taken the competitive edge out of the game. Teams have been bribed to lose matches; players have been substituted during a match, or turned out for three different teams in the same season; organisations hire players and sideline them to prevent other teams from recruiting them. Such actions have reduced first-class cricket in Pakistan to a farce. It is only because Pakistan possesses an abundance of natural talent that we continue to find players of Test calibre. But in the Test arena, talent is not enough. Players are under no pressure in domestic games and there is little opportunity to develop the toughness of mind required in Test matches, particularly on tour. This is why Pakistani teams tended to crack in tight situations. For a number of years we lost every close match, Test or one-day, largely through a failure of nerve. The more competitive the first-class game, the easier it is to prepare oneself psychologically for the rigours of Test cricket. I played in the final of the Sheffield Shield, for New South Wales against Queensland, and the match was as tense as a Test. At the end of the game some players had tears in their eyes.

In a misguided attempt to make the game more professional, the BCCP handed it over to commercial organisations. One former BCCP president, A. H. Kardar, later admitted that the system had become a cancer and needed to be restructured. In order to give some players full-time employment, the whole infrastructure of cricket in Pakistan was destroyed. The regional associations were deprived of their best players and became second-rate teams. This is true even of Karachi and Lahore, whose players are littered across various teams: for example, the PIA team is composed almost exclusively of Karachi players. As all these organisations have their headquarters in Karachi and Lahore, the rest of the country has been turned into a cricketing backwater. The few players who do emerge from other areas have to move to these two cities to develop and maintain their game, or to have any chance of playing first-class cricket. At the same time no one bothers to upgrade facilities or look for talent outside Lahore and Karachi.

The system also encourages favouritism and nepotism. It is easier to play for an organisation if you have connections. The management of a bank is obviously far too involved with weightier matters to care much about the succession of similar surnames that crop up in its cricket team. Promising cricketers are dropped and picked at the manager's and the captain's convenience. Wasim Akram was dropped by Lahore Zone, and later chosen by Pakistan. His second first-class game was a tour match in New Zealand. A lot of promising cricketers were not so lucky. Talaat Ali, an opener, played for Pakistan in New Zealand in 1979, making 40 and 61 against Richard Hadlee in the first Test. His reward was to be dropped for the series against Australia and not to be considered at all for the World Cup because he was thought too old at twenty-eight. He was then dropped by PIA after making a hundred and a double-century in the previous match. No reason was ever given, and his place was taken by the son of the PIA selector. Talaat Ali couldn't play for anyone else without giving up his job, so he chose to retire and continue working as a sales promotion officer for Pakistan Airlines at the age of twenty-eight.

Our first-class cricket is so poorly regarded that not even the national selectors take it seriously. If they want to include someone they sometimes point to his first-class record. On the other hand, a player's first-class performances are often disregarded at the selectors' convenience. Shafiq Ahmed, the most consistent run-getter in domestic cricket, was never given an extended run in Test matches. Instead of Shafiq, a young player like Talaat Mirza was taken on tour to India on the strength of a few fifties. The fringe members of the team lived in perpetual fear of being sidelined. The selection process is entirely Machiavellian in character, and any player who doesn't scrape and bow is in trouble. Sarfraz Nawaz, an outspoken and unconventional cricketer, was dubbed an incorrigible troublemaker, not only by the BCCP but by some captains as well. The selection committee found a novel way of excluding Sarfraz from the team to tour India in 1983. It was common knowledge that Sarfraz got match-fit by playing, and hardly ever took any other form of strenuous exercise. He was summoned to the National Stadium at Karachi and told to do a few quick laps of the ground. After the first lap, Sarfraz was obviously struggling. The selectors promptly declared him unfit and Sarfraz, who should have been an automatic choice, never went to India. He had also been dropped in 1979, ostensibly because he had not participated in the domestic first-class competition.

The usual method employed to weed out 'undesirables' in order to make room for favourites and relatives is the 'trial camp'. Up to a hundred players are called to a camp where the selectors make them play in the nets for a few days. At the end of this farce a squad is announced. Peculiar selections and omissions are justified on the basis of form, fitness or the discovery of a new talent. The keen and discerning eye of the selector sifts the abilities of a hundred first-class cricketers during a few days of net practice! One can hardly blame young cricketers for devoting their energies to befriending officials, journalists and influential players. There is no way one can judge the temperament of a player in a net.

The BCCP is reluctant to reform first-class cricket because the present structure gives it absolute control of the players and the game. The BCCP council is equally divided between elected association representatives and nominees of the commercial organisations. The latter are in no way qualified to make decisions about the game. They are basically a retrogressive power bloc, since any rational restructuring would involve curtailing the role of the commercial organisations. These council members are used to threaten players. Players are told that they will lose their jobs unless they fall into line. This happened during the dispute over Test fees in 1976–7 and during the players' revolt against Javed Miandad's captaincy in 1981–2.

The association representatives have at least some knowledge of the game, but their 'elected' status is, to say the least, dubious. They are supposed to be the representatives of local clubs. On paper there are about seventy clubs in Lahore and over a hundred in Karachi, the majority of which are 'dummy' clubs. As there is no league competition in either city there is no way of evaluating or monitoring the activities or membership of these clubs. Once in power, association officials stay in office as long as they possibly can. In effect, BCCP council members have one common and overriding interest – self-perpetuation. This is largely dependent on the performance of the Pakistani team. So long as it does well they are secure and there is little accountability. No questions are asked about revenue, expenditure, selection or the state of domestic cricket. Advertising contracts have been known to be given away for ten per cent of their market value. The organisers print duplicate tickets, selling one set and returning the other to the Board, with the result that sold-out matches often show little profit. A Gujranwala one-day international against West Indies in 1985 yielded a profit of 1.3 million rupees, while the Lahore match, with over twice as many spectators, produced a profit of 40,000 rupees. No enquiry was held into this blatant fraud.

Obedient BCCP officials are made managers on tour; they occasionally use this as an opportunity to have a good holiday, leaving the team to their own devices. The president of the BCCP, a government appointee, is normally an administrator whose duty it is to raise funds for the BCCP. Some BCCP presidents have been efficient workers, while others have had no administrative skills whatsoever. Most are unable to manage cricketing affairs since they have little or no knowledge of the game. A recent president, General Safdar Butt, said he had little time for the game, and admitted that he knew nothing about it. He once asked Abdul Qadir why he bowled off such a short run-up when the West Indian bowlers took such a long start.

The whole structure is extremely shaky. The moment the team loses an important series – to India in 1979–80, or

Australia in 1983–4, for example – the council, the selection committee, the captain and sometimes even the president of the Board are forced to resign. A new group drawn from the same basic pool takes over and nothing much changes. Over the years it has been a nightmare dealing with the BCCP. The Board demands absolute subservience from the players, and I was never the boot-licking type. Long before I became captain I was not particularly popular with the BCCP council members. Early in my career I was the youngest player to take a stand in a pay dispute with the Board. At that time we received only 1000 rupees per Test, and were the lowest-paid cricketers in the world. A. H. Kardar, the then president of the Board, used all kinds of strong-arm tactics but failed to break the spirit of the dissenting players, and eventually gave in under instructions from the government. Years later I was one of the players who rebelled after the Board had issued a statement questioning our loyalty. The orchestrated attack on the Packer players took place between these two incidents.

However, all this was nothing compared with what happened after I had assumed the captaincy for the second time. The BCCP council members were totally unaccustomed to a captain who insisted on having veto powers over selection and was also critical of the whole set-up. Such an attitude threatened the very foundation of the empire they had built. Now that I was selecting the team and producing results they could no longer bully and abuse players. I knew I was walking a tightrope. The moment I failed, embittered cricket administrators would let loose their 'pocket' journalists on me. This is why my Australian tour of 1983–4 was such a fatal error. I should never have gone solely as a batting captain with a question mark still hanging over my fitness. I still did not fully understand BCCP politics, and the support of the then president and secretary lulled my misgivings. In the end I buried my benefactors, aggravated my injury and opened the floodgates of criticism. All this was not out of character, though, as I have always taken risks.

As I described earlier, I nursed my injury for over a year, and it wasn't until the World Championship of Cricket in Australia in 1985 that I felt fit enough to play international cricket again. I regained the captaincy in November 1985 for the one-day competition in Sharjah. Javed had faced severe criticism for his handling of the team in the three one-day defeats to India early in 1985: he chose to relinquish the captaincy; and I was appointed in his place. After Sharjah we were scheduled to face the West Indies in a five-match one-day series at home – an extremely difficult proposition. This was still the great West Indian side that had demolished all opponents for years. It was the toughest assignment I could possibly have had for my comeback as captain. I knew that if I allowed the BCCP to dictate selection, it would be a disaster. The team was still in the process of rebuilding and I wanted players who had the right temperament and were fighters. This series provided the ideal opportunity to discover such players.

In my absence the Board had reverted to normal selection methods, and BCCP officials were not pleased with my attitude. They thought that after the fiasco of the Australian tour and its aftermath I had learnt my lesson and would be more pliable. A confrontation was inevitable, and the manner in which it began is typical of the high-handedness and sheer ignorance of BCCP functionaries.

The secretary of the BCCP was a retired colonel, Rafi Naseem. After leaving the army, he had tried his hand at poultry farming with no success at all. General Azhar, the BCCP president, brought him on to the Board as a favour. Rafi Naseem believed that he knew a lot about cricket. A small-minded, self-righteous man, he loved to throw his weight around. During the series against Sri Lanka a few months previously, a friend of his, Mian Aslam, had been appointed a Test umpire. In Pakistan there is no proper umpires' association, or any working system for umpires. The appointment of umpires is entirely at the discretion of the BCCP secretary.

Mian Aslam was inexperienced and had been openly abused

by Sri Lankan players in the 1985 Test series. In the one-day series against the West Indies a month later he was again appointed for the third match at Peshawar. He declared Larry Gomes run out, correctly as was proved by the television replay. He was abused by a West Indian player for this decision, became extremely nervous and proceeded to give a few incorrect decisions against us. Over lunch, I told Mian Aslam that he should report this player's misbehaviour to the West Indian manager. He answered that no one had abused him and the whole Pakistani team burst out laughing since they had all heard it. At this moment Rafi Naseem walked into the room and I told him that the Board should at least appoint competent umpires. He replied, 'OK, who is your favourite umpire? Who do you want?' I was furious. The series was even and the team had fought hard against a formidable side. I had enough concerns without having to deal with Mian Aslam's umpiring or Rafi Naseem's crass attitude to the game. I asked him to leave the dressing-room.

He came back an hour later, by which time we had lost two wickets and I was padded up to go in next. He called all the players into the dressing-room, closed the door and demanded an apology. He informed me that BCCP officials could do as they pleased and that the captain had no jurisdiction over the dressing-room. He told me that I needed to be put in my place, and threatened that if I did not apologise he would make public my 'activities at night'. I was stunned. The man seemed to be utterly unconcerned about the tense match situation. He would not leave, so I went outside and sat in the pavilion. By this time I was hardly in the right frame of mind to bat. I later informed the BCCP president of this incident and told him I wanted to resign my job, but he assured me it would not happen again.

During the same series another BCCP functionary walked into the dressing-room with his son and asked me to sign the child's autograph book. He wanted me to get the autographs of the rest of the team for his son as well. I was padded up to bat and signed the book, but didn't get up to collect all the other autographs for him. This annoyed him a great deal as he was obviously used to treating players like errand boys. He reported me to the enquiry committee.

The series was tied at 2-2 and I had just been run out at a critical juncture in the decider at Karachi, when Rafi Naseem chose to make another appearance in the dressing-room. I told him to leave and he replied that I needed to be put in my place. I had great difficulty in controlling myself and not hitting him. After the game he handed me a piece of paper which stated that I was no longer captain. Such a decision was not within his jurisdiction anyway, but it was his way of showing his strength. We lost the one-day series 3-2, and the BCCP council thought this was the right moment to attack me. They obviously knew very little about cricket. In the public eye the team had been a great success and had performed beyond their expectations by fighting the West Indies all the way. Nevertheless the BCCP was determined to get rid of me and set up an enquiry committee to look into my actions.

Despite a concerted effort, the enquiry committee failed to make much headway. Some of the players were interviewed by the committee. At one session, Rafi Naseem walked in and told a player to tell the committee that girls used to visit the dressing-room. He was not above concocting anything. The players all stood by me: Mudassar was sounded out about the captaincy but refused it. Rafi Naseem even obtained statements from association officials, whom I had never even met, accusing me of arrogance, while the autograph incident was also cited as an example of my high-handedness. The usual hack journalists tried to whip up a public campaign against me. Nothing worked, so the BCCP was forced to reappoint me as captain for the series against Sri Lanka, though in some ways I wished they had not. The BCCP also passed a law that all members of the council could come to the dressing-rooms whenever they desired.

The Rafi Naseem incident highlighted many of the weaknesses of the present first-class structure: the abuse of power,

the ignorance of Board functionaries, the quality of association officials, the treatment of players, the selection of umpires
and the quality of sports journalism. If they continue, Pakistan
will be unable to maintain its current position in world cricket.
This would be no reflection on our talent, because Pakistan has
a lot of natural ball players, as evidenced by our success in
squash as well as cricket.

We have to tap this vein by reorganising the structure from
top to bottom. Pakistan is not a rich country, and most people
have neither the resources nor access to facilities to be able to
develop their skills. Instead of 'dummy' clubs we should
organise and promote local leagues which would provide a
large pool of players for first-class cricket – something like
Grade cricket in Australia. A genuine league system would also
become the foundation for strong regional associations. The
Wazir Ali League, through which Lahore players were for-
merly selected, does not exist now, so there is no way of
gauging players' performances. At the first-class level it is
imperative that the teams belonging to commercial organisations are disbanded. These companies can easily promote the
game by sponsoring regional sides, as is the case in all other
countries. This would revive public interest in the game and so
automatically ensure competitive first-class cricket. At the
same time, the sponsoring organisation would take care of the
players' livelihoods, as it does at present. The BCCP council
should consist of elected officials, with elections after every
two years or so, thus making them accountable. If the game
reverted to the normal practice of a regional first-class structure, the association representatives in the BCCP would give it
a core of experienced, knowledgeable administrators. There
should never be either an honorary treasurer or an honorary
secretary of the BCCP. It is no longer a job for amateurs, since
cricket has become big business. There is nothing radical about
any of these suggestions – this is the way the game is run
everywhere else. It is time we admitted that we took a wrong
turning and have reached a dead end. The longer the present
situation is allowed to continue, the more difficult it will be to

remove entrenched individuals and groups. Quick and extensive surgery is necessary if we are not to become a second-rate cricket power.

CHAPTER 13

World Cricket

In any period of rapid economic, political and cultural change there are bound to be problems of adaptation. It takes time to understand how such developments will affect a particular activity. Administrators are conservative and are loath to abandon traditional methods and attitudes: those in power are particularly reluctant to endorse required reforms if they threaten their positions. However, if the lag between reality and action is excessively long the new social forces impose changes despite the resistance of the old order. New techniques and methods are introduced but in a haphazard, purely reactive manner.

Decolonisation brought a number of new countries into world cricket, and as time passed the newer Test-playing countries began to make their presence felt on the field and in the committee rooms. At the same time, international and domestic cricket had to deal with complex and powerful market forces that dictated the form of any sport in the post-war era. Two factors – nationalism and finance – provided the framework in which cricket and cricketers had to survive. This meant the end of cricket as it had been played in the heyday of Empire, when the MCC controlled the game and the phrase 'It's not cricket' was sufficient to define all aspects of the game. Cricketers then were either 'gentlemen' or 'players' – amateurs or professionals – with the former firmly in command.

The bodyline controversy was an early indication that times were changing, but the significance of the tour was lost in the furore surrounding the tactics of one man, Douglas Jardine. By the 1950s it should have been apparent that a crisis was developing. All the unresolved problems of today – umpiring, behaviour, professionalism, finances – were there in embryo, but cricket administrators chose to ignore them and to deliver sermons instead.

Perceptive analysts realised that the game had undergone an enormous change. In his cricket classic *Beyond the Boundary*, first published in 1963, the West Indian C. L. R. James wrote:

> Cricketers try to preserve the external decencies. The tradition is still strong. But instead of 'It isn't cricket', now one hears more frequently the cynical 'Why isn't it cricket?' Scarcely a tour but hits the headlines for some grave breach of propriety on or off the cricket field. The strategy of Test matches is the strategy of stalking prey. You come out in the open to attack only when the victim is wounded. No holds are barred . . . wickets are shamelessly doctored. Series are lost or believed to be lost by doubtful decisions and immoral practices, and the victims nurse their wrath and return in kind.

The West Indies, India, Pakistan and New Zealand emerged as teams to be reckoned with, and by the 1970s most Test series were pretty evenly contested. Cricket became a matter of national pride; biased umpiring and press reporting, misbehaviour by both players and crowds, and ill-feeling between sides began to occur all too often. The most controversial issue was always the umpiring. Operating under the pressure of fierce national and local passions, umpires, who are only human, were bound to make errors of judgment.

In cricket, unlike any other sport, the concept of 'the benefit of the doubt' leaves many vital decisions entirely up to the split-second assessment of one man. On slow pitches, with the ball keeping low, this aspect of umpiring becomes still more crucial because of the number of l.b.w. and bat-pad appeals. In the hot-house atmosphere of modern cricket it is not at all surprising that umpires tend to err in favour of the home side, which is also their own team. The combined pressure of intense public emotion and personal affiliation proves too strong. Some cricketers claim that between home and away tours it all evens out in the end, but certain decisions are crucial to the outcome of a series, and can lead to so much bitterness as to cause incalculable harm to cricketing relations between two countries. The dismal events of the 1987 summer and winter series between England and Pakistan can be traced back to David Constant's decision to give Sikander Bakht out caught at short leg at a critical stage of the final and decisive third Test at Headingley in 1982. The television replay clearly showed that the ball was nowhere near the bat.

There are good and bad umpires in every country, but even the better ones are victims of the current situation. Umpires are not saints, nor are they made of steel. They are subject to the same pressures that make players appeal vociferously at every conceivable – and occasionally inconceivable – opportunity. The unanimous roar of a crowd of thousands coupled with screaming, gesticulating fielders is hardly the ideal environment for cool thinking. Marginal decisions invariably go against the touring side, plus a few that aren't so marginal. It is extremely difficult for a team to win on tour unless it is clearly superior, and Test results in the 1980s bear witness to this. This often leads to the anomaly of a side winning at home, after being soundly beaten in the other country. Complaints about umpiring by touring teams in the past twenty years have been so persistent that something must be seriously wrong. Although such complaints have been more frequent in some parts of the world than in others, no country has been spared.

With the help of multiple cameras and the slow-motion replay, television picks up and highlights every umpiring error; it also differentiates between good and bad umpires, while batsmen who hang around when given out will be shown up by the camera. The modern umpire is caught between two opposing forces – the domestic pressures which encourage error, and the technology which reveals them. Many umpires are under the jurisdiction of their cricket control boards and are anxious to please their superiors. For example, on our tour of India in 1987 the umpires were pressured by the administration to resume the third Test at Jaipur although the pitch was still unfit for play. Both had told me that, according to the rules, the wicket was unfit to play, but after some arm-twisting by the administration they decided to go ahead, knowing it was unfair to us. Again, I was somewhat puzzled when the two umpires called me aside for a chat on the morning of the first day of the Karachi Test against Australia in 1982–3. This was my first home series as captain, and I thought they wanted to explain some rule that was in operation. Instead they asked me for instructions. After that I made a point of telling umpires that they should go out and perform their duties as best they could.

In volatile countries like India, Pakistan, Sri Lanka and the West Indies, umpires are sometimes influenced by fear of disapproval within their own communities. In the second Test at Trinidad in 1976–7 Roy Fredericks was run out on 99 but given not out. The umpire, Douglas Sang Hue, later told Mushtaq, our captain, that he had to live there. During the final, decisive and gripping fifth Test at Bangalore in 1986–7 one only had to look at the umpires' faces to see the strain they were under. I felt sorry for them, and wouldn't have exchanged places with them for anything.

Players are subject to similar pressures to perform. They can hardly be blamed for quarrelling with umpires whom they feel to be biased. Sometimes the situation gets completely out of hand, as it did during the West Indies tour of New Zealand in 1979–80, the Pakistan tour of Sri Lanka in 1985–6 and, most recently, England's 1987–8 tour of Pakistan. On all such occasions the touring teams have lost confidence in the integrity of the home umpires. I became convinced of the need for 'neutral' umpires a long time ago, and after the tour of Sri Lanka I was determined to do something about it on the grounds that the umpiring had been totally biased, and we had been told that exactly the same thing happened in Pakistan. It had proved an extremely frustrating tour because we couldn't get anyone out! Wasim Akram and I, both of us inswing bowlers, were operating on seaming wickets and received only one l.b.w. decision in our favour. In the first two Tests, eleven out of the thirty Pakistani wickets that fell were l.b.w., while of the thirty-one Sri Lankan batsmen dismissed, only one was out in this manner. In the second Test a fight very nearly broke out between the umpire and one of our players, and on one occasion a physical confrontation took place between Javed Miandad and a spectator. The whole team told me they wanted to go home; I felt convinced that to continue was only going to harm the relationship between the two countries. As we have seen, we completed the tour only after we had been specifically instructed to do so by President Zia-ul-Haq.

I was also tired of the complaints about umpiring after every home series. When I became captain we beat India and Australia comprehensively at home, and I am proud to say that umpiring was not cited by either losing captain as an excuse for their defeats. Some previous Pakistan captains had claimed that any umpiring bias at home was balanced out in the decisions against us abroad, but I felt that it merely undermined the quality of our performance. As we have seen, in 1986 I persuaded the BCCP to appoint 'neutral' umpires for the home series against the West Indies. It was a close and exciting rubber, and we could concentrate on playing cricket without worrying about umpiring controversies. I wonder what would have been said if play had been called off by Pakistani rather than neutral umpires just when the West Indies had a chance of winning the final Test? We drew the series against a powerful West Indian side which had destroyed all opposition for nearly a decade, yet apart from isolated incidents there were no umpiring problems. This effectively silenced those who had argued that neutral umpires would face the same pressures and not do much better.

No one followed our example. England and Australia in particular were adamant in their opposition to the idea. The 1987 World Cup once again proved that international umpires were an unequivocal success. The cricket bureaucracies in the traditional Test-playing countries remained unimpressed. We saw the disastrous consequences of this ostrich-like attitude in the post-World Cup series between England and Pakistan.

I'm sorry to say that English opinion on this matter reeks of colonial arrogance. English umpires, we are told, are the most experienced, competent and fair in the world; by agreeing to an international panel England would only be discriminating against its own umpires; such a panel, if chosen on merit, would largely consist of English umpires anyway; and so on and so forth. Lurid descriptions of an Ashes Test at Lord's being umpired by an incompetent West Indian and a probably dishonest Pakistani were enough to convince the public: why should England and Australia suffer for others' shortcomings? This blinkered and self-serving approach was exposed at Faisalabad, when confrontation between Mike Gatting and Shakoor Rana threatened to curtail the series and ruin relations between the two countries. As a result some influential voices in England belatedly spoke up in favour of 'neutral' umpires. Unfortunately, it takes a major crisis to prod the cricket establishment into trying to come to terms with current realities.

The same colonial mentality, operating in a post-colonial world, was responsible for another major crisis that almost split the cricketing world. By the 1960s it was obvious to an intelligent schoolboy that the newly independent countries would not tolerate racial discrimination. Although racial and ethnic prejudices are present throughout the world, the systematic and legalised brutalisation of coloured people in South Africa is unacceptable to anyone who believes in human rights. The Third World nations have a clear view on apartheid and believe there should be a complete embargo on South Africa. Apartheid is an all-embracing system which includes racial discrimination in sport. The English cricket establishment should have realised that their relations with South Africa would eventually anger the coloured cricket-playing countries. However, far from keeping their distance from South Africa, they actually refused to select Basil D'Oliveira to go on tour there because the South Africans had threatened to call it off if a black man was chosen. This was not just appeasement, it was collaboration. There were such widespread protests in England that eventually the selectors had to include D'Oliveira, which led to the cancellation of the tour. The D'Oliveira affair should have taught them something about the worldwide distaste for sporting relations with South Africa, yet many years later, when the West Indies, India and Pakistan opposed to the inclusion of players who had gone on an unofficial tour of South Africa, the TCCB sanctimoniously objected on the grounds that no other country could dictate selection. It was even argued that to punish players for earning a living in South Africa was a curtailment of individual rights.

I am not suggesting that anyone can or should stop a player from going to South Africa, but that the player should know that he is exchanging a Test career for financial security. There can be no compromise on this, because coloured nations are going to find it progressively harder to swallow hypocritical arguments about the freedom of the individual. Apartheid is the yardstick by which commitment to human rights is measured, and cricket is not a holy cow that is above fundamental principles. I was amazed when a majority of members at a Cricketers' Association meeting in England supported those players who had gone to South Africa.

Whereas apartheid, which is opposed by the vast majority of the world's population, was not considered a sufficient cause to ban players immediately, the Packer issue led to quick and decisive action: all the Packer players were banned from Test cricket without a word about individual rights. Yet the various boards never stopped to think that they had been largely responsible for creating Packer. It was not until the early 1960s that cricket administrators tried to deal with the financial requirements of the game. The cost of staging first-class and Test matches had escalated rapidly, while the number of spectators at first-class matches had decreased. With much heel-dragging and moaning about the decline of traditional values the one-day game was introduced.

A few years later it was realised that this was not enough, and that the sport needed corporate sponsorship to generate sufficient funds. These changes, although necessary, were carried out by men who basically disapproved of them. The modernisation of cricket was in the hands of administrators from another age, with neither the temperament nor the financial acumen for the job. It was Kerry Packer's organisation, with its hard-headed marketing approach, that took the sport into the late twentieth century – night cricket, coloured clothing, revolutionary television coverage, protective gear and the elevation of cricketers to star status. Packer created a marketable product, exciting and glamorous. Since this revolution occurred outside the confines of the first-class and Test structure, its perpetrators had no qualms about highlighting certain aspects which attracted spectators but which, in the long run, were not good for the game. An overdose of hype and aggression was injected into cricket.

It is easy to blame Packer's World Series Cricket, but the truth is that the cricket establishment had not seriously tried to find a financial solution, and were quite willing to take over what Packer had wrought once the crisis was over. As far as the players were concerned, the Packer years were a godsend. Until then cricketers had been paid a pittance for their efforts. The cost of living and salaries in other sports had increased dramatically, while cricketers, even Test players, were hardly paid a living wage. The Packer crisis bulldozed the boards of each country into making players' salaries rather more commensurate with the money that they generated, although cricketers are still underpaid compared with golfers, tennis players or footballers, to name but a few. However, the elevation of outstanding performers to star status by the media enabled them to augment their earnings by promoting products. First-class players in general, and not only Test cricketers, benefited. The same Cricketers' Association which had supported players with South African connections was quick to demand a ban on all Packer players from county cricket. The English side went one step further and refused to play if Pakistan included their Packer players in the third Test at Karachi in 1977–8. The BCCP buckled under pressure and – as mentioned earlier – Mushtaq, Zaheer and myself, having flown in from Australia specially for this Test, were excluded from the Pakistan team.

Packer marketed the one-day game aggressively and made it into a real moneyspinner. After World Series Cricket the cricketing administration in Australia just took over and were happy to reap the bonanza. From Australia to Sharjah, one-day cricket keeps the money flowing. The cricket establishment has made no attempt to find a proper equilibrium between the one-day game, Test cricket and first-class cricket. There are too many tours packed in each year, and Test cricketers are being worn out prematurely. The overdose is apparent. In Pakistan there was no enthusiasm for the 1987–8 English tour after the non-stop excitement of the World Cup; in India in 1986–7 Pakistan were squeezed in after Australia and Sri Lanka at the end of a single season.

I enjoyed the kind of life we led enormously when I started touring in 1971 – playing cricket, staying in top-class hotels, being entertained by one's hosts. It was a wonderful life, and there was always time off between matches to go sightseeing or to the beach. As a result, it was quite a relief to finish at Oxford. From now on I would be free to travel all year round, all over the world. I always treated cricket tours like paid holidays and considered myself extremely lucky that it was supposed to be my profession as well. The only real problem with touring life was the lack of companionship, in that I spent most of my cricketing career among players with whom I had nothing in common except cricket. Our interests and outlooks on life were totally different. Even so, I mixed much more easily with my team-mates than did my two cousins, Majid and Javed Burki. I only learned about Javed's being a recluse when I came into the Pakistan team after he had retired. Despite the age difference between us Majid and I shared rooms, and I used to look up to him like an elder brother. But we led completely different lives. I had some great moments during my career with Sarfraz, Mudassar, Javed and Qadir, but we all went our own ways once the tours were over.

Touring life changed after Kerry Packer's World Series and the emergence of one-day cricket. Tours gradually became more and more hectic. For the first time matches were played against several touring teams in the same season, and more and more one-day internationals were squeezed into every tour. In the 1987–8 tour of India, the West Indies played eight one-day internationals, as well as four Test matches. All this means that players have hardly any time to relax, as they are either recuperating from the strenuous one-day matches or travelling to different destinations. Present-day tours have lost a lot of their charm for me.

A tour now consists of Test matches, a number of one-day internationals and a few side games as well. In the long term, one-day games take much more out of a player than Test cricket. The demands on both mind and body are enormous, with the result that top players are now picking and choosing their tours. The absence of stars devalues matches, but it is inevitable with the current non-stop round of fixtures. At the same time, the first-class season has expanded, with a host of one-day competitions on top of the usual three- or four-day fixtures. In England in particular the cricket is non-stop. On top of all the travelling, a county cricketer has a seven-day week. If this goes on, the cricketing life of a player will be drastically reduced. This would be unfortunate, because players mature with age and are at their best in their thirties. Something has to be done before outstanding players start dropping out of the game early, as is happening in tennis.

There should also be some rationale behind the planning of tour itineraries. Most importantly, one-day internationals should take place after the Test matches. The five-day game is slower and more complex, and requires a lot of patience on the part of spectators. Some Test matches are bound to be dull draws. The public's appetite should not be jaded by the helter-skelter excitement of the one-day game before the Test series begins. At the same time, tour organisers should keep the

1, 2. Great all-rounders: *above* Mike Procter, Kapil Dev

3, 4. *Below*, Richard Hadlee, Sir Garry Sobers

5, 6. Great captains and great batsmen: *Above*, Ian Chappell and Greg Chappell with Rodney Marsh; *below*, Viv Richards and Clive Lloyd

7, 8, 9, 10. Great batsmen: *Top left:* Geoff Boycott; *top right:* Gordon Greenidge; *below left:* Barry Richards (the wicketkeeper is Farokh Engineer); *below right:* Allan Border

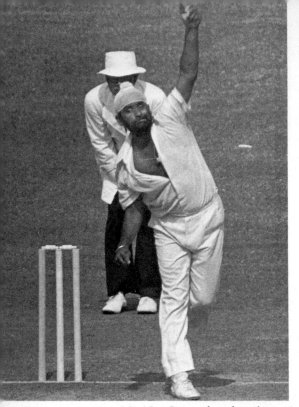

11, 12. Great slow bowlers: *Top left:* Bishan Bedi; *top right:* Derek Underwood

13, 14. Great wicketkeepers: *Bottom left:* Rodney Marsh (the batsman is Geoff Boycott); *bottom right:* Alan Knott

15. Great fast bowlers: Dennis Lillee

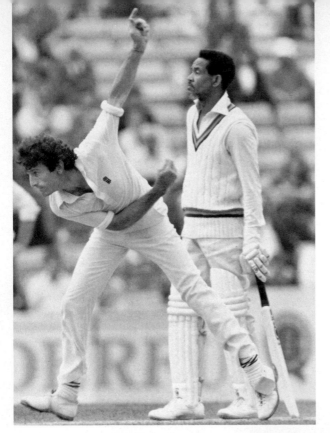

16. John Snow

17. Jeff Thomson

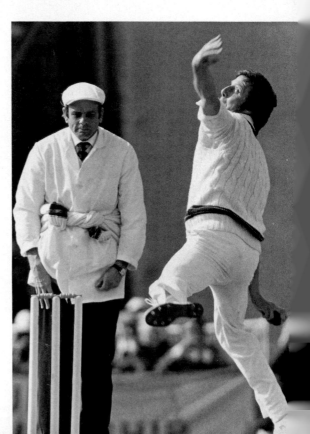

18. Andy Roberts

19. Malcolm Marshall

20. Joel Garner

21. Michael Holding

players' welfare in mind, and not just the financial rewards. In India there were so many games in such a short period that I lost half a stone because of the heat and non-stop travelling: other players lost even more, not to mention their injuries. There must be some enjoyment left in the game: cricketers are not machines in a production line.

The worst aspect of this commercialisation is that Australia is hogging the cricket season from November to February. Because they pay more money, teams go to Australia in the height of the Australian season and visit the sub-continent during our off-season, when it is hot and the pitches are brown and placid, fast bowlers' graveyards. This is the sort of thing that the ICC should regulate; they should see to it that poor countries do not get a bad deal. There must be something seriously wrong with the overall planning of tours in world cricket if – for example – Pakistan only toured the West Indies twice in thirty-five years, as was the case until this year.

Cricket has acquired stars, glamour, sponsorship and a highly charged atmosphere: everything that goes with modern sport. If it is to keep some of the essentials that make it unique, a lot of hard thinking will have to be done. The most important thing is to guide the development of the game in such a way as to bring it into harmony with the world around it. There is no essential discrepancy between the game's time-honoured virtues and the world we live in. It is a matter of creatively adapting the form in order to preserve the content. So far much valuable time has been wasted on quibbling over what 'isn't cricket', and not much has been devoted to what cricket should become.

On the whole the media have been kind to me. I have no complaints about the press anywhere except in Pakistan. Touring cricketers all over the world are generally treated well by the press: the problems arise at home, where regional loyalties can lead to a bad press that may have nothing to do with actual performances on the field. As a sportsman I am quite prepared to accept criticism when I do badly, just as I am happy to be praised for a good performance. As my own most severe critic, I don't even read the papers when I have played badly, but what I find hardest to take is a planned campaign against me reflecting nothing more than regional bias. I first became aware of this when I was made captain in 1982. Javed Miandad was seen as a Karachi boy who had been toppled by the Lahore lobby because the entire team had refused to play under him. Once I became captain, I became the target of a planned campaign by certain Karachi journalists. To begin with I felt confused. I had heard about Karachi and Lahore lobbies in the team, but I had never actually come across them. They were not present at BCCP level, but were always evident in the press. I had never thought of myself as representing any particular city while playing for Pakistan, and I was amazed at how Qadir's selection was immediately attacked as an attempt to dislodge a Karachi spinner, Iqbal Qasim.

As a result of the campaign by those Karachi journalists, a section of the Karachi crowd also turned against me. The abuse at the ground took much of the pleasure out of playing in the highly responsive conditions of the Karachi stadium. When the news broke in 1983 that I would not be playing in the World Cup due to the stress fracture in my leg, a leading Karachi daily, the *Star*, carried a headline to the effect that I had sold out to the bookies – and this was just after I had achieved a Pakistan record by taking forty wickets in a home series. From then on I realised that there was no point in worrying about it, because I would be attacked whatever I did. I thought about taking the paper to court, but was advised against it, the libel laws in Pakistan being virtually non-existent. Any attempts I made to discourage people at the Karachi stadium from running onto the field were seen as discrimination against Karachi crowds. This meant that, in order to avoid criticism, other players were friendly to hooligans who ran onto the field – so encouraging more to follow suit.

The sad thing is that the masses believe what appears in the papers, no matter how often one contradicts it. I have been engaged to be married — according to several Pakistan papers — to four different girls in one year! Statements are attributed to me in my absence, with the result that every summer, while playing county cricket in England, I am told about what I am supposed to have said in the Pakistani papers.

In England and Australia the libel laws are relatively strong, but one has to be fairly rich to afford the legal fees. On one occasion I wanted to sue a cheap sensational English paper which had published a story about me. My lawyer told me that I should be prepared to spend up to £200,000. One can only hope that people will see through such sensational stories.

Luckily I'm not one of those people in the public eye who feels shocked when his private affairs appear in the papers. That is extremely naive. One should be discreet about those aspects of one's life that one would prefer not to see in the papers. I do hate it, though, when failure on the field is attributed to alcohol, womanising, politics or gambling — more often than not because some sports journalist in Pakistan doesn't have a good enough understanding of the game to present a proper critical analysis. Intrigue is much easier, and sells the papers. With more newspapers in the market, the standards of journalism have improved. When I started out I was amazed at the power some journalists had over the players. Most players would lick the boots of journalists for a good write-up. One journalist threatened to end a player's career after the player had run off with his girl friend.

CHAPTER 14

All Round View

My political views were influenced by my parents, in that I too am patriotic and anti-colonial. However, unlike my parents' generation, I am not anti-Indian. My generation did not witness the struggle to create Pakistan and the bloodshed at the time of Partition in 1947. The more I toured India, either playing for Pakistan or taking part in some charity match, the more I realised that most people on both sides of the border wanted a good relationship between the two countries. The suspicion and animosity created by border disputes and two full-scale wars have been a great burden on both countries. In Pakistan defence spending accounts for 65 per cent of our budget, leaving hardly any room for much-needed expenditure on health and education, which barely amount to 4 per cent. India has high defence spending too, and I am sure that, given the poverty there, it desperately needs to be reduced.

The founder of Pakistan, Mohammed Ali Jinnah, was trying to buy land in Simla – a hill station in India – three weeks before Partition. He envisaged Indo-Pakistan relations as being rather similar to those between the USA and Canada. I wonder if he ever anticipated an arms race between the two countries. Any politician in either country who wants instant popularity can rely upon taking an anti-Indian or an anti-Pakistan line to do the trick. It may be naive to hope that one day India and Pakistan will have the kind of relationship envisaged by Jinnah, but it is essential for the development of both countries. Perhaps the post-Partition generations in both countries will come to see the futility of confrontation, and that the arms race is a luxury we can do without. I also feel strongly that we should be non-aligned. We should never let ourselves be drawn into a super-power conflict, like the Afghan civil war.

There are so many real problems in Pakistan to which we should be addressing ourselves. At the moment we have the highest population growth rate in the world, and if this continues we are going to have severe problems in the next twenty years; yet nothing is being done about it. Urban land prices have already shot up, way beyond the reach of salaried people. In the northern areas, population growth has led to massive deforestation, and this has caused considerable soil erosion and other ecologically damaging changes.

Throughout the country health care is in a bad state, which is not surprising given that barely 2 per cent of the budget is allocated to it. Three years ago, when my mother was suffering from cancer and in considerable pain, I came into contact with our hospitals for the first time. I was horrified. I suddenly realised how fortunate the English are in having the National Health Service, whereby anyone can walk into a hospital and be treated. The poor in Pakistan have no such luck, and even the rich struggle to receive proper attention.

One day I went to buy some medicine for my mother. While I was waiting for the pharmacist to bring it to me, an old man rushed in with a prescription. I recognised the expression on his face at once: it was exactly the same as the look I had seen on the faces of my sisters and father when my mother had a spasm of pain brought on by her cancer. He showed the prescription to the pharmacist, and asked how much the medicine would cost. When he heard the price, his expression revealed the obvious truth: he didn't have enough money for it. He told the pharmacist to hold on to the prescription while he went to find some. Later the pharmacist told me that the man's brother was dying of chest cancer and in great pain. Although the old man had managed to pay for a bed in Mayo Hospital, he had run out of money for medicine. When my own medicine arrived, the pharmacist took me aside and told me that as a special favour he had given me an imported brand as the local ones were not that effective.

This had a traumatic effect on me. I suddenly realised that the sick, and especially the poor, have no chance in Pakistan. Subsequently I had the misfortune to visit a children's ward in Multan, and felt ill for days after seeing three to four children in one bed. When my mother died of cancer I decided that I would raise funds for a hospital for the poor once I had given up cricket, and since the World Cup I have been working on some ambitious plans to this end.

Equally distressing is the widespread corruption in our society, which is more or less institutionalised. If one sets up in business, one has to make allowances in the costings for bribes. In Pakistan today one can only be honest if one can afford to be. My first cousin, who is a police officer, had to have money sent to him by his mother, because his salary was not enough for him to maintain a decent standard of living. An ordinary policeman earns a basic pay of 975 rupees (£30) per month, on which he is expected to maintain a family. Unless he is corrupt, it is impossible for him to live decently. Because of inflation, salaries have fallen way behind, and it is partly for this reason that corruption has become so much a part of our way of life. As a result, nationalisation policies cannot be expected to work in Pakistan. A revolutionary change in our social structure – especially in economic terms – is needed if we are to rid ourselves of this menace.

Politically the country seems to be drifting towards fragmentation. The minority provinces feel that they are being exploited by the Punjab and the Centre. The solution to this may well be decentralisation, breaking up the country into several smaller provinces, each of which runs its own health, education, welfare and law and order, rather like individual states in America.

And no matter how naive this may sound, I would like to see disarmament take place, not only between India and Pakistan, but worldwide. I see no difference between money made out of arms trading and that which is made through the drug trade. Both are evil.

The two outstanding decisions I have taken during my life were not to drink alcohol and not to get married. I really believe that marriage and cricket are incompatible. I don't see how anyone can do justice to his wife and kids if he's on the move all year round. Some tours last as long as four months, and they must put tremendous pressure on any marriage. Nor does it really help when wives come on tour for a few weeks: most players are completely caught up in the game, and it must make the wives feel uneasy to see female fans hovering round their husbands, particularly if they happen to be attractive men. I know of various cricketers who were reluctant to tour because they realised that they were missing out on family life. When he made himself unavailable for an overseas tour, Greg Chappell was quoted as saying that he wanted to be with his children when they were growing up. A lot of county crick- eters' wives complain that they have hardly any family lives: their husbands are either playing cricket or recovering from it. Moreover, the life of a professional sportsman is riddled with insecurity, including the drama of retirement from the game and starting a new life. I am sure I would look at life after cricket with much more apprehension if I had a wife and kids: I would have to look to their security first, and might well find it impossible to choose something that would suit me.

When I was leaving for England with the Pakistan touring team in 1971, my mother's last words were 'Don't bring back a foreign wife'. There were two reasons for her fear of inter- racial marriage: she felt that to expect a Western girl to adapt to our culture was asking far too much, and that sooner or later the marriage would break up; and that there was always a chance that if she found it impossible to settle in Pakistan she would take me back with her. As a result, I always assumed that I would follow in the footsteps of my older cousins, three of whom went to Oxbridge and came back to arranged marriages in Pakistan.

I would have got married had I not set off on the inter-national cricket bandwagon, with the result that I was never long enough in Pakistan to get roped in. When I reached the age of thirty I felt that the time had come for me to settle down, and that if I left it any later the age gap between the girl and myself would be too great. However, all this proved much easier in theory than in practice.

Just as I was becoming reconciled to the idea of an arranged marriage, I became involved with an English girl. Despite all the arguments about the long-term impracticality of such a relationship, I began – to my own surprise – to contemplate marriage to her. I then realised that, where emotions are concerned, there is no room for logic. Sad to say, cultural differences and the touring life combined to end our rela-tionship, but it taught me that I could no longer be sure how, when or whom I would marry.

I believe that whether one makes an arranged marriage or a love marriage, one has to work hard to make it succeed. Arranged marriages have a greater chance of success because expectations are low and family pressures from both sides make the couple try harder; and Pakistani society is conducive to family life. The problem with a love marriage is that if one partner falls out of love, there is not that much left to sustain it. What makes marriages work is companionship, which can come out of an arranged marriage or a love marriage. As in life, a lot of luck is required to make a marriage succeed.

The people I feel sorry for are the Pakistanis who have settled in Britain. They seem very confused. The younger generation has been brought up in English schools and adopted Western ideas, while their parents insist on Eastern values. The greatest problems arise when Western-educated girls have their mar-riages arranged with men from villages in Pakistan, with whom they have nothing in common. Maybe this will sort itself out by the next generation.

Whether the Pakistani immigrant community will have been assimilated into the English society by the next generation is another matter – and here they seem equally confused. They are often subject to racial prejudice, which makes them want to belong to Pakistan, but because they have grown up in England, they now have no roots there. They are almost as alien in Pakistan as the English. One of my Pakistani friends who had lived all his life in England came to Pakistan for the World Cup: he ended up with severe stomach problems, and doesn't think he will go back again. Younger generation Pakistanis are different from their parents in that they are not apologetic about living in England. They are conscious of their rights and much more aggressive. Since 1971 I have seen a change in the behaviour of the Pakistani supporters on the Test grounds – but, sadly, I often feel they come to the grounds more to prove a point than to enjoy the cricket. Perhaps they want to prove to the English that they're equals.

My older sister always told me I was ugly as a boy, which I accepted after cursing my luck for a while: in any case, cricket and shooting were much more important to me at the time than looking good. Indeed, so involved was I in my life that my worried mother asked my older sister one day whether I was a normal child. So it came as a pleasant surprise when I first began to be thought of as good-looking. I suspect that this coincided with my cricketing success.

I am constantly amazed at the amount of fame I have attracted, since I have always thought of myself as no more than a cricketer who has achieved a certain amount of success. I'm not complaining about it: there is no greater satisfaction for any sportsman or entertainer than to be appreciated. My parents and my sisters always played down my fame. Whenever I boasted of success at home, both my parents would quote from the Quran that 'all honour and disgrace is in the hands of Allah'.

I became famous for the first time on the Indian tour of 1979, and I kept assuming that I had been mistaken for someone else. It was then I discovered that a team will tolerate one player having all the limelight so long as he can produce the goods. The moment he can't live up to what is expected of him, resentment sets in. When I was injured, and couldn't perform, I became the target of a lot of snide remarks from my team mates and our press. Fame adds greatly to the pressure on a player, and if he fails to live up to his image, the criticism begins to pile up.

Because cricket is such a glamour sport in the sub-continent, I acquired greater fame within the two countries than would have been the case had I played for England. Being recognised everywhere may well be enjoyable to an extrovert, but, being shy, I find all the public attention uncomfortable. I particularly dislike being recognised in a crowd.

My father, who first learned I was good at cricket when he heard on the news that I had been selected to play for Pakistan, always played down my fame. One day I went with him to look at the harvest on his lands near Mian Channu. Whenever I tried to stay clear of crowded places on the way there, he told me that I had an inflated opinion of my fame, and that it had all gone to my head. Despite my reluctance, he insisted that we ate at a crowded restaurant near the rest-house where we were spending the night. Next morning we were woken up by a panic-stricken *chowkidar* who insisted that unless I came out the front door would be broken down. When I did so, I found that there were thousands of people waiting outside. My father was genuinely bewildered. He had not realised that television had spread cricket to even the remotest areas of Pakistan.

One thing that my parents managed to drum into me was that, no matter how famous one becomes, one's feet should remain firmly planted on the ground; that all adulation is temporary, and public memories are short.

Pakistan v West Indies
1988

When I retired from Test cricket in the first week of November, I began to do all those things that cricket had prevented me from doing. Since the cricket season in Pakistan coincided with our shooting season, from the age of eighteen I had been unable to pursue my great passion in life: camping in the wilderness and shooting. So I went shooting in some of the remotest areas of Pakistan, accepting from old school friends invitations which I had been unable to accept before.

When I decided to go to the West Indies on 18 January, I reckoned it would take me three weeks to get fit. We had two and a half weeks of training camp before we embarked on the training tour. What I had not realised was that, at the age of thirty-five, three months of no cricket and no training had taken a heavy toll of my fitness. Because I have to leap to get into my bowling action, my body has to be in perfect condition for me to bowl at my best. To make matters worse, Abdul Qadir had kidney problems, while Wasim Akram was a doubtful starter for the tour after a groin operation. But by far the greatest worry for me was the tour itinerary. Our second match was to be a one-day international, followed by four others and a side match before the first Test. After the first Test there was a three-day match, followed by two Tests with only two days' rest between each of them, during which we had to travel. It was a crazy itinerary, obviously designed to maximise profits at the expense of the players. Mainly as a result of itineraries like this, the West Indian and Pakistan players decided to form a Cricketers' Association which would insist that when future itineraries were made, a players' representative would be present to safeguard their interests.

We started the tour disastrously. In the first one-day international Tauseef Ahmed was injured and had to be sent home. Moreover I found that my body was still not strong enough to take the jarring on the hard West Indian wickets, and I played the first three matches with a back strain. Predictably we were destroyed in the one-day series, losing 5–0 – and I was hit all over the place.

The team's morale was really low, and I found it hard to raise it since I was struggling myself. My fitness became a source of great worry to me. Just as my back was getting stronger, I received a thigh injury which not only left me extremely frustrated, but made me wonder whether I was getting too old to bowl fast. One night, returning to the hotel after being thrashed about the park, my body aching all over, I actually wondered whether I would ever be fit and on form again. I've always believed that one can do anything in life as long as one doesn't give up mentally, but now I was unable to convince myself that I could.

I could see similar doubts on the faces of my team members. Tours like this test one's ability as a captain to the ultimate. Two things really kept me going: the team depended on me so much, particularly at this stage; and my pride was hurt by the cricket fans saying that I shouldn't have come to the West Indies because I was past it. One can always tell when a team's morale is down by their reluctance to practice. When England were on their last, disastrous 5–0 tour, the worse they performed the more time they spent on the beach. Our manager, Intikhab, suggested that if we gave them some more rest days, they might become more enthusiastic. I've always been against this kind of thinking, which seems to me to be a form of escapism. There's only one way to improve one's performance, and that is to practise and work on one's weaknesses. Throughout the tour we practised, even on our rest days during Test matches. We had two practice sessions a day. I gave most of the batsmen special practice sessions in short-pitched bowling by throwing wet tennis balls at them from a distance of eighteen yards: this was to develop a technique for coping with the short ball, as well as sharpening their reflexes. It also prepared them mentally for the Test matches.

Fortunately, just before the first Test my aches and pains began to ease, and I knew I was getting stronger. Although Richards and Marshall had pulled out of the first Test through injuries, our morale was still low after the hammering we had taken in the one-day matches. On the morning of the first Test I started to feel a pain in my toe. I was desperate to win the toss and bat, hoping that it would be better by next day, but I lost the toss and the West Indies batted. I started tentatively, and gradually the pain disappeared as I warmed up. By the end of the first day we had bowled them out for 290, with my getting 7 wickets. Next day I could hardly walk; I found I had a severe toe infection and was put on heavy doses of antibiotics. It was lucky that I had bowled first, as I would not have been able to do so for the next three days. We got over 400 runs, thanks to a highly intelligent century by Javed. Shoaib and Javed took the sting out of the West Indian pace attack by leaving alone three or four bouncers an over. Salim Yousuf, supported by the tail, attacked the flagging West Indian pace-bowlers. Having a lead of almost 150 put the West Indian batsmen under tremendous pressure. My toe had three days' rest in which to recover, and although I felt weak after the infection and high doses of antibiotics, I was not going to let anything get in the way of victory. Qadir bowled brilliantly in the second innings. He took three wickets, and I managed four; Wasim had a thigh injury and hardly bowled at all.

It was a great win after being so down throughout the tour. Even though we knew that Richards and Marshall were to play in the next two Tests, the team felt confident.

Our next two Tests were incredible in terms of both tension and the quality of the cricket – one-day matches can never really reach the same kind of climax as great Test matches. As far I was concerned, there was drama even before the second

Test began. I strained a leg muscle during fielding practice a couple of days before the Test was due to begin. In forty-eight hours there was no improvement at all. On the eve of the match I saw two specialists, both of whom felt that if I wanted to play in the third Test – which was to begin two days after the second Test had ended – I should not play. They felt I was only half-fit anyway, and that there was a chance of the injury being aggravated during during the match. If it got worse, not only would I be unable to bowl in the second Test, but I would miss the third Test altogether.

This put me in a real quandary. I kept the news a complete secret from the team, but I had a meeting with Intikhab and Javed. Both felt that I had to play for the sake of team morale – even if it meant doing so only as a batsman. I had a sleepless night trying to work out all the things that could go wrong. I had taken such risks in the past – during the first Test against England at Manchester in 1987, for example – and I had been severely criticised when they had backfired.

Fortunately, when I started training on the morning of the Test the muscle felt a little better. I bowled a couple of overs of medium pace in the nets, and felt the pain reach a certain level and stay there, rather than getting worse. I decided that I would risk going into the match as a bowler.

We won the toss and put them in – a great gamble, since we went in with only two pacemen, Wasim and I, both of whom were carrying injuries. My experience of the Trinidad ground was that after two days it became a spinner's wicket, so I thought that the spinners could take care of the second innings if Wasim and I managed to contain them in the first. Wasim began by bowling possibly the fastest spell of the series on a moist wicket. Meanwhile I got Gordon Greenidge out in the first over, bowling medium-paced inswingers. After five overs Wasim broke down again, leaving the attack looking fragile on a wicket that was still helping seamers and giving no assistance to spinners. It was then that Qadir bowled a magnificent spell, attacking as well as stock-bowling from one end. In my second spell I bowled faster, and we ended up getting the West Indies out for 174 by tea-time – Qadir and I taking four wickets apiece.

I was extremely pleased, feeling sure that the spinners, Qadir and Ijaz Faqih, would put immense pressure on the West Indians once we had got a big lead – and by now the wicket was playing well. I also felt happy that my gamble had paid off.

By the end of the day all my hopes of a big first-innings lead were shattered – we were 5 down for 50. Next day we managed to get a 20-run lead, mainly due to gutsy innings by Salim Malik and Yousuf. By the close of play they were 50 ahead with three wickets down. My worst fears had come true. Wasim was only bowling medium-pace with the help of pain-killers, and our off-spinner, Faqih, had injured his index finger and could not bowl. I bowled 45 overs in the second innings, but these included some of my best spells in Test cricket. I got the first five wickets and the West Indies were facing defeat on several occasions, but things didn't go our way. We didn't help ourselves by dropping catches. Our fielding had always been a source of worry to me. Despite extra fielding practices it has let us down on many occasions – such as at the Oval on the last day of the series against England in 1987. Pakistan cricketers tend to neglect this aspect of the game, relying only on team practices to improve their fielding. English cricketers work much harder in this department.

Unfortunately one of the umpires was of the kind that believed in avoiding criticism by not giving any decisions. I felt I had Richards l.b.w. twice. The first time could have been crucial, as the West Indians were four wickets down and only 70 ahead, and I was still fresh: had he been given out I would have gone through the rest, as I was in the middle in one of my best spells in Test cricket. With only two and a half bowlers, the longer they battled on the more our bowling lost its sting. It was hot and humid and the wicket was getting slower. It didn't turn at all, so Qadir was becoming ineffective as the bounce became lower.

Eventually the West Indies set us 372 to win. Javed got another 100, minimising risks and just accumulating runs. We needed 80 to win off 20 overs, with 5 wickets in hand; it seemed as though the match was ours. Then Richards brought himself on and had Ijaz Ahmed stumped. Javed was out next over, and the match again hung in the balance. When Wasim was out, I asked the batsmen to play for a draw with ten overs left. Richards brought himself back for the last over, and for once the same umpire decided to give a decision – Salim Yousuf was l.b.w. off the first ball. Qadir played out the last five balls amid great tension. I couldn't even watch that last over.

Everyone in the Caribbean predicted that the Barbados Test would be won by the West Indies in three days: after all, they hadn't lost there since 1935. When Viv won the toss and put us in to bat on a green wicket the crowd roared as if the match was won. But a score of 99 for 1 in the first session made everyone realise that perhaps this Test was going to be different to others played at Barbados. We got 309 and bowled out the West Indians for 307. At various stages both teams were poised for huge totals but collapsed. The story was repeated in the second innings where we looked set for a score of over 350 but struggled to 262. When they came in to bat it looked as if they would overtake our modest total by the end of the fourth day. In fact they collapsed too, and in the end needed 60 with two wickets left. They got it amid great tension.

Both Marshall and Wasim bowled superbly in this match. Marshall showed his class, always bowling to a plan, mixing pace with control. Wasim bowled faster on occasions than any other bowler on either sides. Shoaib batted well for us. He is an intelligent, hard-working and gutsy cricketer and on this tour he looked a much improved player. The other batsman who stood out for us was Salim Yousuf. He is one of the gutsiest cricketers I've ever played with. Despite being hit in the face and breaking his nose in the first innings, he came back and played a vital innings of 28 in the second.

Qadir bowled well but seemed a frustrated man when the tour ended. Most batsmen don't read him at all and play him by simply thrusting their front feet down the wicket. This makes them vulnerable to his flipper – which is like a finger spinner's arm ball. Unfortunately most umpires don't know the difference between a flipper and the rest of Qadir's armoury. He would lay a trap over the space of two to three overs, only to find that when he had the batsman trapped, the umpire was as surprised as the batsman. He even resorted to warning the umpire before bowling his flippers.

If we want legspinners to come back into Test cricket, we will have to raise the standards of umpiring; and this brings me back to the taboo subject of umpires. It was such an epic series – the best I've ever played in – that it deserved to be supervised by the two best umpires in the world. For most of the series the umpiring was excellent. Even the one umpire who was not competent was still consistent. Problems occurred when the last two Tests entered their crucial stages. In the second Test Yousuf was given l.b.w. on the front foot by an umpire who was scared to take any other decisions at all. And in the last innings at Barbados, when the West Indies needed 80 runs with 3 wickets left, Qadir had two decisions in one over turned down. The first was a flipper that got Marshall when his foot was still coming out, and two balls later Dujon – who went on to win the match for the West Indies – snicked a ball onto his pad and was caught at short leg. The snick could be heard in the stands. Everyone stood in disbelief, since that umpire was considered to be one of the best in the world and until then we all had a great respect for his judgement. There could easily have been a nasty incident since by then the players were under so much pressure and tension. I had to hide my intense disappointment and tell the boys to keep on going – realising that incidents on cricket fields can have far-reaching repercussions, like the Gatting–Rana affair.

In many ways, this was worse than dealing with a consistently bad umpire, like the one in Trinidad, because this was such a crucial moment in the match. The standard of umpiring had been so consistently high that we could only conclude that, in this case, patriotism had taken over. From that point on our entire team lost confidence and respect for him. This was not the first time I'd seen previously impeccable umpires sway towards the home team during the crucial stage of a match. In Bangalore in the second innings, for example, Ramaswamy, whom we had previously thought very highly of, gave Gavaskar – on whom the match depended – not out caught off his glove. The moment we got him out we won the match by a margin of sixteen runs – and the series. I have a great deal of sympathy for the umpire, even so: when the same West Indian umpire gave Greenidge out l.b.w. in the first innings of that last test, he was booed by the crowd. The fairest thing for all concerned would be neutral umpires. Even though England has the most professional umpires, I'm afraid that for the sake of world cricket it is imperative that an international panel should be formed. After all, they have them in all other professional sports, so why not in cricket?

Sadly Qadir, who is a highly emotional man, seemed to wilt after that over. His frustration was taken out on a spectator, who had been abusive to all our boundary line fielders. His bowling deteriorated noticeably after that. I should have taken him off, but kept thinking he would lift himself after an over or so.

I have to say that I would never have forgiven myself if I had missed this series. The team gave me their complete support, even if I was disappointed by our fielding and, on occasions, by our batting. But now that county cricket is closed to our batsmen, our domestic cricket is an inadequate basis on which to build Test temperament in our batsmen. Javed was the only one in the top order who seemed unscathed by one-day cricket.

Javed also gave me his complete co-operation. He is an out-and-out team man who tries to help on and off the field. My respect for him went up during the series. Both he and Mudassar also gave me useful help in the field. A bowling captain often gets involved in his own bowling and needs help from senior players. Intikhab, the manager, was excellent and took a lot of pressure off me – especially when I was struggling during the early part of the tour.

I was disappointed by my batting on the tour, since I feel that at the moment my batting is better than ever before – so to fail in this department was particularly annoying. However, getting back to bowling fitness, and then bowling as a stock and attacking bowler in the first two Tests, took a lot out of me, with the result that my concentration on batting was not as good as it should have been against such high-class pace-bowling. I was also disappointed that I couldn't support Wasim at Barbados during the second innings. But, relying as I do on a huge leap before getting into my bowling action, I need firm ground to take off from as well as to land on. Unfortunately in the second innings – and even, to some extent, in the first – the foot-holds were completely broken, and I was unable to bowl with pace or control.

Nevertheless, by drawing the series in the Caribbean and beating both England and India on their home grounds, Pakistan is now considered the best team in the world together with the West Indies. I only wish that we had played a five Test series, supervised by the world's two top umpires, to decide which was the greatest team in the world. Anyway, if it is the last Test Series I ever play, what a way to go!

Imran Khan in Test Cricket

Statistics by Steven Lynch of Wisden Cricket Monthly

Batting and Fielding

Season	Opponents	Venue	M	I	NO	Runs	HS	Av	100	50	Ct
1971	England	E	1	1	–	5	5	5.00	–	–	1
1974	England	E	3	6	1	92	31	18.40	–	–	2
1976–7	New Zealand	P	3	4	1	105	59	35.00	–	1	1
1976–7	Australia	A	3	5	–	86	48	17.20	–	–	2
1976–7	West Indies	WI	5	10	–	215	47	21.50	–	–	2
1978–9	India	P	3	4	2	104	32	52.00	–	–	–
1978–9	New Zealand	NZ	2	3	1	63	33	31.50	–	–	–
1978–9	Australia	A	2	4	–	90	33	22.50	–	–	1
1979–80	India	I	5	8	1	154	34	22.00	–	–	–
1979–80	Australia	P	2	2	–	65	56	32.50	–	1	–
1980–1	West Indies	P	4	7	–	204	123	29.14	1	–	–
1981–2	Australia	A	3	5	1	108	70*	27.00	–	1	1
1981–2	Sri Lanka	P	1	1	–	39	39	39.00	–	–	1
1982	England	E	3	5	1	212	67*	53.00	–	2	–
1982–3	Australia	P	3	3	2	64	39*	64.00	–	–	1
1982–3	India	P	6	5	1	247	117	61.75	1	–	4
1983–4	Australia	A	2	4	1	170	83	56.67	–	2	–
1985–6	Sri Lanka	P	3	2	–	69	63	34.50	–	1	–
1985–6	Sri Lanka	SL	3	4	–	48	33	12.00	–	–	4
1986–7	West Indies	P	3	6	2	115	61	28.75	–	1	1
1986–7	India	I	5	7	2	324	135*	64.80	1	2	–
1987	England	E	5	5	1	191	118	47.75	1	–	3
1988	West Indies	WI	3	5	1	90	43*	22.50	–	–	1
			73	106	18	2860	135*	32.50	4	11	25

* denotes 'not out'

Record against each country

Country	M	I	NO	Runs	HS	Av	100	50	Ct
England	12	17	3	500	118	35.71	1	2	6
Australia	15	23	4	583	83	30.68	–	4	5
West Indies	15	28	3	624	123	24.96	1	1	4
New Zealand	5	7	2	168	59	33.60	–	1	1
India	19	24	6	829	135*	46.06	2	2	4
Sri Lanka	7	7	–	156	63	22.29	–	1	5
	73	106	18	2860	135*	32.50	4	11	25

Record on Pakistan grounds

Ground	M	I	NO	Runs	HS	Av	100	50	Ct
Iqbal Stadium, Faisalabad	6	7	1	286	117	47.67	1	1	1
Niaz Stadium, Hyderabad	2	1	–	13	13	13.00	–	–	4
National Stadium, Karachi	9	13	4	313	63	34.78	–	2	2
Gaddafi Stadium, Lahore	9	11	3	384	123	48.00	1	1	1
Ibn-e-Qasim Bagh Stadium, Multan	1	1	–	10	10	10.00	–	–	–
Jinnah Park Stadium, Sialkot	1	1	–	6	6	6.00	–	–	–
	28	34	8	1012	123	38.92	2	4	8

Record in each country

Country	M	I	NO	Runs	HS	Av	100	50	Ct
Pakistan	28	34	8	1012	123	38.92	2	4	8
England	12	17	3	500	118	35.71	1	2	6
Australia	10	18	2	454	83	28.38	–	3	4
West Indies	8	15	1	305	47	21.79	–	–	3
New Zealand	2	3	1	63	33	31.50	–	–	–
India	10	15	3	478	135*	39.83	1	2	–
Sri Lanka	3	4	–	48	33	12.00	–	–	4
	73	106	18	2860	135*	32.50	4	11	25

Record when captain

	M	I	NO	Runs	HS	Av	100	50	Ct
Record when not captain	40	62	7	1399	123	25.44	1	4	11
Record when captain	33	44	11	1461	135*	44.27	3	7	14
	73	106	18	2860	135*	32.50	4	11	25

Centuries in Test cricket (4)

123	v West Indies	Lahore	1980–1
117	v India	Faisalabad	1982–3
135*	v India	Madras	1986–7
118	v England	The Oval	1987

fifty and five wickets in an innings in the same Test

56 and 7–52	v England	Edgbaston	1982
67* and 5–49	v England	Headingley	1982
77, 6–98 and 5–82	v India	Faisalabad	1982–3

Captaincy

Season	Opponents	Venue	M	W	L	D	Toss won
1982	England	E	3	1	2	–	2
1982–3	Australia	P	3	3	–	–	2
1982–3	India	P	6	3	–	3	3
1983–4	Australia	A	2	–	1	1	1
1985–6	Sri Lanka	SL	3	1	1	1	–
1986–7	West Indies	P	3	1	1	1	2
1986–7	India	I	5	1	–	4	4
1987	England	E	5	1	–	4	2
1988	West Indies	WI	3	1	1	1	1
			33	12	6	15	17

Bowling

Season	Opponents	Venue	M	Balls	Runs	Wkts	Av	BB	5wI	10wM
1971	England	E	1	168	55	0	–	–	–	–
1974	England	E	3	672	258	5	51.60	2–48	–	–
1976–7	New Zealand	P	3	908	421	14	30.07	4–59	–	–
1976–7	Australia	A	3	964	519	18	28.83	6–63	3	1
1976–7	West Indies	WI	5	1417	790	25	31.60	6–90	1	–
1978–9	India	P	3	·973	441	14	31.50	4–54	–	–
1978–9	New Zealand	NZ	2	663	255	10	25.50	5–106	1	–
1978–9	Australia	A	2	752	285	7	40.71	4–26	–	–
1979–80	India	I	5	914	365	19	19.21	5–63	2	–
1979–80	Australia	P	2	336	144	6	24.00	2–28	–	–
1980–1	West Indies	P	4	540	236	10	23.60	5–62	1	–
1981–2	Australia	A	3	902	312	16	19.50	4–66	–	–
1981–2	Sri Lanka	P	1	314	116	14	8.29	8–58	2	1
1982	England	E	3	1069	390	21	18.57	7–52	2	–
1982–3	Australia	P	3	620	171	13	13.15	4–35	–	–
1982–3	India	P	6	1339	558	40	13.95	8–60	4	2
1983–4	Australia	A	2	–	–	–	–	–	–	–
1985–6	Sri Lanka	P	3	724	271	17	15.94	5–40	1	–
1985–6	Sri Lanka	SL	3	696	270	15	18.00	4–69	–	–
1986–7	West Indies	P	3	638	199	18	11.06	6–46	2	–
1986–7	India	I	5	739	392	8	49.00	2–28	–	–
1987	England	E	5	1010	455	21	21.67	7–40	2	1
1988	West Indies	P	3	779	416	23	18.09	7–80	2	1
			73	17137	7319	334	21.91	8–58	23	6

Record against each country

Country	M	Balls	Runs	Wkts	Av	BB	5wI	10wM
England	12	2919	1158	47	24.64	7–40	4	1
Australia	15	3574	1431	60	23.85	6–63	3	1
West Indies	15	3374	1641	76	21.59	7–80	6	1
New Zealand	5	1571	676	24	28.17	5–106	1	—
India	19	3965	1756	81	21.68	8–60	6	2
Sri Lanka	7	1734	657	46	14.28	8–58	3	1
	73	17137	7319	334	21.91	8–58	23	6

Record on Pakistan grounds

Ground	M	Balls	Runs	Wkts	Av	BB	5wI	10wM
Iqbal Stadium, Faisalabad	6	1300	558	22	25.36	6–98	2	1
Niaz Stadium, Hyderabad	2	500	174	11	15.82	6–35	1	—
National Stadium, Karachi	9	2148	838	49	17.10	8–60	2	1
Gaddafi Stadium, Lahore	9	2027	803	50	16.06	8–58	3	1
Ibn-e-Qasim Bagh Stadium, Multan	1	192	89	5	17.80	5–62	1	—
Jinnah Park Stadium, Sialkot	1	225	95	9	10.56	5–40	1	—
	28	6392	2557	146	17.51	8–58	10	3

Record in each country

Country	M	Balls	Runs	Wkts	Av	BB	5wI	10wM
Pakistan	28	6392	2557	146	17.51	8–58	10	3
England	12	2919	1158	47	24.64	7–40	4	1
Australia	10	2618	1116	41	27.22	6–63	3	1
West Indies	8	2196	1206	48	25.13	7–80	3	1
New Zealand	2	663	255	10	25.50	5–106	1	—
India	10	1653	757	27	28.04	5–63	2	—
Sri Lanka	3	696	270	15	18.00	4–69	—	—
	73	17137	7319	334	21.91	8–58	23	6

Record when captain

	M	Balls	Runs	Wkts	Av	BB	5wI	10wM
Record when not captain	40	10247	4468	175	25.53	8–58	11	2
Record when captain	33	6890	2851	159	17.93	8–60	12	4
	73	17137	7319	334	21.91	8–58	23	6

Bowling – *cont.*

Ten wickets in a Test match (6)

12–165	v Australia	Sydney	1976–7
14–116	v Sri Lanka	Lahore	1981–2
11–79	v India	Karachi	1982–3
11–180	v India	Faisalabad	1982–3
10–77	v England	Headingley	1987
11–121	v West Indies	Georgetown	1988

Picture Credits

Picture Credits

The author and publishers would like to thank the following for permission to reproduce photographs:

Section One

Plates 7, 14, 15, 16, 17: Patrick Eagar; plate 6: S & G Press Agency Ltd; plate 11: *Oxford Mail and Times*.

Section Two

Plates 1, 2, 3, 4: All-sport/Adrian Murrell; plate 5: Patrick Eagar.

Section Three

Plates 1, 2, 4, 5, 10, 14, 16: All-sport/Adrian Murrell; plates 3, 6, 7, 8, 9, 11, 15: Patrick Eagar; plate 12: *Sports Week*; plate 17: Adrian Murrell; plate 18: Iqbal Munir.

Section Four

Plates 2, 3, 4, 5: Patrick Eagar; plate 6: All-sport.

Section Five

Plates 1, 10: Topham Picture Library; plate 2: Nikhil Sportsworld, Calcutta; plates 4, 5, 7, 8, 11: Patrick Eagar; plates 6, 9: All-sport.

Section Six

Plates 1, 2, 3, 5, 9, 11, 12, 17, 18, 19: Patrick Eagar; plates 4, 6, 7, 10, 13, 14, 15, 16, 20, 21: Adrian Murrell; plate 8: All-sport/Adrian Murrell.

Acknowledgements

The author and publishers wish to thank the following for permission to reproduce photographs: Mushtaq Ahmed; Chris Cole/Allsport; Patrick Eagar; Santosh Ghosh/Sportsweek; Iqbal Munir; Adrian Murrell/Allsport; Nikhil/Sportsworld, Calcutta; *Oxford Mail and Times*; Royal Grammar School, Worcester; Emma Sergeant; Sport and General. All other photographs are from Imran Khan's personal collection. Every attempt has been made to trace the copyright in photographs, but in some cases this has not proved possible.

The quotation from *Beyond the Boundary* by C. L. R. James is reproduced by kind permission of the author and the Century Hutchinson Publishing Group.

The author would like to thank Azhar Karim; the author and publishers would like to thank Gabrielle Allen for the picture research, and Steven Lynch of *Wisden Cricket Monthly* for editorial assistance and the statistical summary.

Index